DATE DUE

DE 08 05			
J-20-09			

Fairy
Tales

THE GREENHAVEN PRESS COMPANION TO
Literary Movements and Genres

Fairy
Tales

Jann Einfeld, *Book Editor*

David L. Bender, *Publisher*

Bruno Leone, *Executive Editor*

Bonnie Szumski, *Editorial Director*

Stuart B. Miller, *Managing Editor*

David M. Haugen, *Series Editor*

Greenhaven Press, Inc., San Diego, CA

Every effort has been made to trace the owners of copyrighted material. The articles in this volume may have been edited for content, length, and/or reading level. The titles have been changed to enhance the editorial purpose. Those interested in locating the original source will find the complete citation on the first page of each article.

Library of Congress Cataloging-in-Publication Data

Fairy tales / Jann Einfeld, book editor.
    p. cm.—(Literary movements and genres)
  Includes bibliographical references and index.
  ISBN 0-7377-0416-0 (pbk. : alk. paper)—
  ISBN 0-7377-0417-9 (lib. bdg. : alk. paper)
  1. Fairy tales—History and criticism. I. Einfeld, Jann.
II. Greenhaven Press companion to literary movements
and genres

PN3437 .F35 2001
398.2—dc21   00-29389
                                                            CIP

Cover photo: Circa Art

Copyright ©2001 by Greenhaven Press, Inc.
PO Box 289009
San Diego, CA 92198-9009
Printed in the U.S.A.

"Deeper meaning resides in the fairy tales told me in my childhood than in any truth that is taught in life."

Johann Schiller,
German Poet
(1759–1805)

CONTENTS

Chapter 2: Writers and Collections of Fairy Tales

Chapter 3: Analyzing Fairy Tales

Chapter 4: Influence on Literature

Chapter 5: Assessment of the Genre

FOREWORD

The study of literature most often involves focusing on an individual work and uncovering its themes, stylistic conventions, and historical relevance. It is also enlightening to examine multiple works by a single author, identifying similarities and differences among texts and tracing the author's development as an artist.

While the study of individual works and authors is instructive, however, examining groups of authors who shared certain cultural or historical experiences adds a further richness to the study of literature. By focusing on literary movements and genres, readers gain a greater appreciation of influence of historical events and social circumstances on the development of particular literary forms and themes. For example, in the early twentieth century, rapid technological and industrial advances, mass urban migration, World War I, and other events contributed to the emergence of a movement known as American modernism. The dramatic social changes, and the uncertainty they created, were reflected in an increased use of free verse in poetry, the stream-of-consciousness technique in fiction, and a general sense of historical discontinuity and crisis of faith in most of the literature of the era. By focusing on these commonalities, readers attain a more comprehensive picture of the complex interplay of social, economic, political, aesthetic, and philosophical forces and ideas that create the tenor of any era. In the nineteenth-century American romanticism movement, for example, authors shared many ideas concerning the preeminence of the self-reliant individual, the infusion of nature with spiritual significance, and the potential of persons to achieve transcendence via communion with nature. However, despite their commonalities, American romantics often differed significantly in their thematic and stylistic approaches. Walt Whitman celebrated the communal nature of America's open democratic society, while Ralph Waldo

Emerson expressed the need for individuals to pursue their own fulfillment regardless of their fellow citizens. Herman Melville wrote novels in a largely naturalistic style whereas Nathaniel Hawthorne's novels were gothic and allegorical.

Another valuable reason to investigate literary movements and genres lies in their potential to clarify the process of literary evolution. By examining groups of authors, literary trends across time become evident. The reader learns, for instance, how English romanticism was transformed as it crossed the Atlantic to America. The poetry of Lord Byron, William Wordsworth, and John Keats celebrated the restorative potential of rural scenes. The American romantics, writing later in the century, shared their English counterparts' faith in nature; but American authors were more likely to present an ambiguous view of nature as a source of liberation as well as the dwelling place of personal demons. The whale in Melville's *Moby-Dick* and the forests in Hawthorne's novels and stories bear little resemblance to the benign pastoral scenes in Wordsworth's lyric poems.

Each volume in Greenhaven Press's Companions to Literary Movements and Genres series begins with an introductory essay that places the topic in a historical and literary context. The essays that follow are carefully chosen and edited for ease of comprehension. These essays are arranged into clearly defined chapters that are outlined in a concise annotated table of contents. Finally, a thorough chronology maps out crucial literary milestones of the movement or genre as well as significant social and historical events. Readers will benefit from the structure and coherence that these features lend to material that is often challenging. With Greenhaven's Literary Movements and Genres in hand, readers will be better able to comprehend and appreciate the major literary works and their impact on society.

INTRODUCTION

One would be hard-pressed to find a genre more in need of scholarly focus than the beleaguered fairy tale. Tales like "Cinderella" and "Beauty and the Beast," which have been told and retold for over a thousand years by adults for adults, have been sanitized, distorted, and dismissed as mere children's bedtime stories. "In this century at least," says English professor Roger Sale, "so many people know fairy tales only through badly truncated modern versions, that it is no longer really fairy tales they know."[1]

Fairy tales have a long and distinguished heritage. "Cinderella" has been found in over seven hundred variants all over the world, dating back to the ninth century in China. Popular versions of the fairy tale are thin remnants of an oral tradition. Oral variants of "Cinderella" tell of a bold and forthright heroine who, through perseverance, ingenuity, and grace under pressure, meets the conditions necessary to break the spell that has kept her true and noble nature hidden. It is a deep and haunting tale of the stripping away of illusion and recovery of the authentic self. Similarly, early versions of "Snow White" are not about a wicked queen's jealousy of the young heroine; instead, they focus on the envy of Snow White's mother as her daughter begins to blossom into early womanhood. Furthermore, Little Red Riding Hood in the older tales is not saved by a passing woodsman, or eaten by the wolf, but rather escapes certain death by adopting her perpetrator's tactics of cunning and deception. Even Sleeping Beauty is awakened by a suckling child whom she has conceived while in her long sleep rather than by a charming prince. Most of these famous fairy tales differ from the popular conceptions of them and contain much more profound messages.

AN INFLUENTIAL ART FORM

Once an ancient oral art form in which storytellers held small groups spellbound recounting wondrous tales, fairy tales now represent a mass-media phenomenon of awe-inspiring proportions and dominion. Fairy-tale novels, movies, television series, commercials, cartoons, toys, and video games saturate the world of adult and child alike. *How Fairy Tales Shape Our Lives* is the subtitle of a work published by Sheldon Cashdan in 1999. And "shape our lives" they do. Psychologist Eric Berne says fairy tales not only influence people's hopes and dreams but also can be actual programs for their behavior. "Cinderella, I liked best," said a twenty-six-year-old divorced mother of two interviewed by folklorist Kay Stone. "She was gorgeous. I was homely, and I kept thinking it would happen to me too—I'd bloom one day. But it's never happened. I'm still waiting!"[2] Danish author Isak Dinesen says she is able to live her life more bravely because she reads the fairy tales of Hans Christian Andersen. Fairy tales can free and empower people or constrain and constrict them, sending them on long misplaced journeys in search of fulfillment. They are a major socialization tool and cultural determinant in contemporary Western civilization. Thus, to read and understand them requires an alert and discerning eye.

THE LEGACY OF FAIRY TALES

Fairy tales present the quintessential conflict between good and evil. Since the beginning of recorded time and probably beyond, they have been, in the words of scholar Jack Zipes, "a means to conquer the terrors of mankind through metaphor."[3] William Shakespeare, Charles Dickens, Charlotte Brontë, Nathaniel Hawthorne, Thomas Mann, Oscar Wilde, Edgar Allan Poe, Anne Sexton, and many other writers of distinction have drawn on the metaphorical muscle of the genre to comment on their society or to present their view of a better world. Fairy tales are allied with hope and a utopian spirit. They suggest that change is possible and miraculous transformation is entirely plausible. They implant noble notions of valor, compassion, and essential goodness. A legacy of the fairy tales of childhood is the idea that a small and seemingly inadequate hero can take on overwhelming adversity and emerge triumphant.

Folklorists, professors of language and literature, psychiatrists, historians, librarians, writers, storytellers, parents, and educators continue to debate the nature, meaning, function, and significance of the fairy tale as genre. According to British folklorists Iona and Peter Opie, fairy tales have caused more controversy than any other form of traditional literature since Jacob and Wilhelm Grimm published their famous collection in the early nineteenth century. This book presents a small sample of this large and vibrant body of scholarship.

THEORIES OF ORIGIN

Most famous fairy tales come from the oral storytelling tradition. The question of the origins of fairy tales has intrigued scholars since the discipline of folklore was founded in Europe in the early nineteenth century. Early studies focused on trying to find a rational explanation for the fantastic content of fairy tales.

British antiquarian Edwin Sidney Hartland and folklorist Andrew Lang asserted that fairy tales represent the worldview of prehistoric man. This included a belief in the separation of body and spirit, meaning that spirits could exit one body and occupy another and that certain people had the power to effect such transformation. Fairy tales helped primitive man comprehend the vast and inexplicable forces of nature by imbuing the birds, beasts, sun, moon, earth, and sky with spirits that exhibited human passions and personalities. Other scholars, like folklorist Ruth Benedict, refute the need for a rational explanation of the genre's origin, claiming that fairy tales are the eternal expression of a wild and fanciful imagination freed by the wish-fulfillment characteristic of the tales themselves.

A number of other theories of fairy-tale origins have been advanced. In 1859, following the discovery of Sanskrit as the parent of European languages, German scholar Theodor Benfrey claimed that all classical fairy tales were based on ancient Indian folklore texts. The *Panchatantra,* written in Sanskrit in the third century, incorporated several animal tales thought to be antecedents of modern European fairy tales like "Puss-in-Boots." This theory was discredited with the discovery of records of fairy tales preserved on papyrus dating back as far as 2000 B.C. in ancient Egypt and references to tales of fairies, monsters, and marvels in *Wasps*, written by the Greek playwright Aristophanes in 422 B.C.

Since the mid-1800s, many other theories have been advanced. In 1870 George Cox of the School of Solar Mythology claimed that fairy tales were early man's poetic rendering of the conflict between the Sun and the darkness of night. Hungarian psychological folklorist Geza Róheim believed the source of many tales was dream material. Russian folklorist Vladimir Propp of the myth-ritual school of origins said fairy tales arose from primitive rites and myths, often secret tales containing tribal wisdom and sacred knowledge that were passed on by the elders during initiation rites. For example, British folklorist E.D. Phillips suggested a link between sacrificial rites practiced by tribes in Siberia and Robert Southey's tale known as "Goldilocks and the Three Bears." In order to appease the angry ghosts of bears killed for ritual sacrifice, Siberian tribesmen built three wooden huts in the forest and placed the bear pelts in them. The myths supposedly became detached for the rite and floated into the oral tradition as tales of magic.

Folklorists have also been fascinated by the prevalence of very similar oral fairy tales throughout the world. In 1893 British folklorist Marian Cox published her analysis of 345 versions of "Cinderella" found in widely divergent parts of the globe that had no known early contact with each other. To explain the multiple existence of fairy tales, some scholars have claimed that the same dreams, concerns, and fantasies are common to all of humankind and thus similar expressions of stories spontaneously arise from the psychic unity of all people. Refuting the psychological approach, Diffussionists believe the multiple existence of folktales is based on historical fact, on the movements of sailors, merchants, gypsies, and early traders. In the late nineteenth century Finnish scholars Kaarle and Julius Krohn argued that the life history of each major fairy tale must be explored individually. They traced the history and movement of specific tales and suggested a place and date of origin for many of the most famous ones, insisting that the originators of the tales were lost to history. "The history of fairy-stories," says fantasy writer J.R.R. Tolkien in his classic essay "On Fairy-Stories," "is probably more complex than the history of the human race, and as complex as the history of human language. All three things: independent invention, inheritance and diffusion have evidently played their part in producing the intricate web of story. It is now beyond all skill but that of the elves to unravel it."[4]

THE CIVILIZING FUNCTION OF EARLY LITERARY FAIRY TALES

By most accounts the first literary tale, a clear antecedent to modern fairy tales, is "Cupid and Psyche," written in Latin by Lucius Apuleius in the second century. It is considered the root tale of "Beauty and the Beast" and was part of a larger work called *Metamorphoses* (also known as *The Golden Ass*), which is the story of a young man who is turned into an ass by magic. Some scholars believe "Cupid and Psyche" was based on a cult initiation myth about the Egyptian goddess Isis and was a product of Apuleius's interest in the religious initiation rites associated with the goddess's worship. It has been suggested that Apuleius was initiated into that cult, which was one of the reasons why the parents of his betrothed accused him of casting a spell over their daughter to entice her to marry him. "Cupid and Psyche," a tale that subscribed to such mesmerization, is thought to have some autobiographical content as well as being based on oral folklore and earlier Latin texts.

Another work in Latin, produced in about 1300, was *Gesta Romanorum,* which consisted of anecdotes and tales (including tales of magic) and was used principally by the clergy to impart morals to their charges. It is said to have influenced the work of Shakespeare and English poet Edmund Spenser, who wrote "The Faerie Queen," a famous poem of the sixteenth century that drew on fairy-tale motifs and themes.

One Thousand and One Arabian Nights, first recorded in Arabic in about 1500, comprises oral tales from Arabia, Egypt, Persia, and India. It consists of the frame story of Scheherazade, the wife of a violent and merciless king, who stays her own execution night after night by amusing the king with fairy tales. Through cunning, compassion, and the messages in the fairy tales, she succeeds in civilizing the bestial drives of her husband while at the same time imparting lessons in Muslim customs and law to the audience. Antoine Galland's elegant reworking of the Arabic text into French in 1717 had a significant impact on the format, style, and motifs of the European fairy tale as genre. Writers of fairy tales still employ the device, attributed to the influence of *One Thousand and One Arabian Nights,* of setting their tales in faraway lands to discuss sensitive issues at home.

These early literary tales did not stand as individual stories but were included within frame stories with other types of tales. Unlike the oral tales on which they were based, the literary tales focused on teaching values and ethics to males in preparation for powerful roles in society. "Whereas many of the oral fairy tales were concerned with the humanization of natural forces," writes Professor Zipes, "the literary fairy tale, beginning with 'Cupid and Psyche,' shifted the emphasis more toward the civilization of the protagonist who must learn to respect special codes and laws to become accepted in society and/or united to reproduce and continue the progress of the world toward perfect happiness."[5]

The frame story persisted in fairy-tale literature for years, influencing even Renaissance scholars and storytellers. Italy was at the forefront of cultural developments during the Renaissance, a time when humanism looked to the rebirth of a lost human spirit and the classical wisdom that had been neglected during the Middle Ages. It is not surprising then that the first European storybook to include fairy tales for a mixed audience of upper-class men and women was Gianfrancesco Straparola's *The Pleasant Nights,* published in two volumes in 1550 and 1553. This consists of a frame story in which Straparola and a group of political dissidents forced to flee Milan pass their evenings in exile telling each other jests, tall tales, and fairy tales. In 1634 another Italian author, Giambattista Basile, wrote *Lo cunto de li cunti (The Tale of Tales),* also known as *Pentamerone,* which was the first European attempt to frame an entire collection of fairy tales based on oral folklore. The work includes early variants of "Cinderella," "Snow White," "Sleeping Beauty," and "Beauty and the Beast."

SUBVERSIVE FRENCH BEGINNINGS

France's place as a central power in Europe with a rich and innovative cultural life and technological advances in printing were contributing factors to the development of the literary fairy tale in the late seventeenth century. The Italian fairy tales circulated throughout the courts of Europe and captured the attention of the aristocratic women of the French salon. Many of the tales were similar to fairy tales told by French nannies emerging from a common oral tradition. Yet in the intellectual salons, fairy tales served both as a diversion from the grim realities of life and as a venue to covertly express discontent with the policies of Louis XIV. Expensive foreign wars meant high taxes, which curbed the extravagant lifestyle of the elite. A heavy death toll in combat, combined with serious crop failure, led to much social unrest. This historical context shaped the early character of the genre, as the tales could be readily interpreted as political commentary on the state of the nation.

In the salons of Paris, where elite women and men met to discuss art, politics, literature, and love, the genre was first named *contes de fée,* or fairy tales. Zipes suggests that the imprint of the fairies on the naming of the genre was significant in determining its evolution. For the first time the power of metamorphosis was placed in the hands of women, "the redoubtable fairies." Against the backdrop of two centuries of burning witches at the stake for nonconformism, women were not free to speak openly of alternative beliefs to those of the established church and monarchy. These could be safely expressed in a symbolical code in fairy tales. In fact many beliefs that went against the grain of traditional religion, social conventions, or the monarch's law could be disguised in fantasy in the world of fairies. "There was something subversive about the institutionalization of the fairy tale in France during the 1690's," says Zipes, "for it enabled writers to create a dialogue about norms, manners and power that evaded court censorship and freed the fantasy of the writers and readers while at the same time paying tribute to the French code of civilité and the majesty of the aristocracy."[6]

Provocative, often bizarre, and extraordinary salon fairy tales flourished between 1690 and the early part of the next century. "The Utopian impulse was not much different than the Utopian impulse that led peasants to tell their folktales," says Zipes, "but the wish fulfillment in the oral tales of the peasants arose out of completely different circumstances of oppression and hope. The salon tales were marked by the struggles within the upper classes for recognition, sensible policies and power."[7] Once considered vulgar and not worth the attention of the elite, folklore was elevated in tone and style by writers like Marie-Catherine D'Aulnoy, who wrote *The Island of Happiness* and subsequently published four volumes of fairy tales between 1696 and 1698. D'Aulnoy was the foremost fairy-tale teller in her day and was considered the innovator of the fairy tale as literary genre. The influence of "Cupid and Psyche," early Italian literary tales, and French folklore was evident in her work along with her use of the genre to express political concerns. In the main tale of her first collection, the hero Adolph fails to achieve total happiness as he sacrifices love for glory in war, which was a covert condemnation of the king's aggressive wars abroad and the incredible sacrifices demanded of his subjects.

CHARLES PERRAULT'S MORAL PURPOSE

A frequent visitor to the French salon and confidante of D'Aulnoy, Charles Perrault published his *Mother Goose Tales* in 1697. Many versions of the most famous fairy tales read by children today, such as "Cinderella," "Sleeping Beauty," and "Little Red Riding Hood," are based on Perrault's stylish renditions. His central purpose in writing the tales, however, was less related to producing a children's text and more to do with winning support in a famous intellectual debate of the time.

The son of a member of the French Parlement, Perrault acquired a position under an influential politician and pursued a successful administrative career promoting the arts and sciences. But his real love was his writing and poetry. Perrault struggled most of his career trying to establish credentials amongst the literary elite. In 1697, in an attempt to appease his critics, he published a long poem called "The Age of Louis the Great." While the aim of the poem was to flatter the king and Perrault's contemporaries by suggesting the superiority of modern society over ancient times, it inadvertently sparked a famous intellectual debate known as the "Quarrel of the Ancients and Moderns."

Charles Perrault stood firmly on the side of the "moderns" who believed France's progress depended on developing a culture of enlightenment based on the beliefs of the common people and the wisdom conveyed through their folklore. Perrault took these folktales and added a specific moral dimension. In the preface to the third edition, he writes, "I believe that my fables are more worthy of being recounted than most of the ancients' tales . . . which were created only to please, without regard for sound morals, which they greatly neglected."[8] And so the real audience of his *Mother Goose Tales* was the literary establishment, which could appreciate the subtle way he transformed well-known fairy tales into moral treatises. Perrault's opponents felt his position denounced the classical literary tradition of the great authors of antiquity, such as Homer and Virgil, and amounted to pagan worship. According to Jeanne Morgan Zarucchi, Perrault's biographer, the debate had far-reaching implications, providing the impetus for the revolutions of the eighteenth century and justifying the abolition of outmoded social systems. Ultimately, Louis XIV declared in favor of the wisdom of the ancients, and Perrault's personal and artistic credibility suffered by being linked to this conflict forevermore.

FAIRY TALES ARE CONVENTIONALIZED AS CHILDREN'S LITERATURE

Contrary to popular belief, the literary fairy tale for children was not established by Charles Perrault, although his *Mother Goose Tales* achieved fame and recognition far in excess of the works of the women of the French salon. It was not until the publication of Governess Le Prince de Beaumont's "Beauty and the Beast," fifty years later, when more widespread acceptance of the fairy tale as a literary genre had taken place, that it was to be considered appropriate literature for children.

In 1740 Madame de Villeneuve, another product of the French salon, published an elaborate version of "Beauty and the Beast" based on Apuleius's "Cupid and Psyche." Seventeen years later Governess de Beaumont reworked and simplified Villeneuve's "Beauty and the Beast" with the express purpose of conveying standard notions of proper behavior to her charges. This led to a more widespread acceptance of the literary form as appropriate for adults and children of all social classes. Coupled with the large-scale distribution of *bibliothèque bleue,* or cheap chapbooks, in France in the eighteenth century, the literary fairy tale, once the sole purview of the elite intellectual, went back to the masses to interact with the oral tradition and became an established literary form for children.

In 1789 Charles Mayer published forty-one volumes of fairy tales, which included most of the French fairy tales from the preceding century. With this publication the genre became firmly established in the Western intellectual tradition. This meant that all future writers of fairy tales borrowed from an established literary convention.

GERMAN ROMANTICISM AND THE FAIRY TALE

Developments in Germany provided the next impetus in the institutionalization of the fairy tale as a genre in the Western world. Under the influence of the French tales, German Romanticists like Novalis, Ludwig Tieck, and E.T.A. Hoffman took the European fairy tale to new horizons. In their hands, the genre underwent a major shift in function to become a vehicle for the critique of the ideology of the aristocracy and social institutions. Johann Wolfgang Goethe's "The Fairy Tale" (1795) denounced the harsh aspects of the Enlightenment and the French Revolution. In the late eighteenth and early nineteenth centuries, a further shift in the genre occurred to include social commentary. "The evil forces assume a social hue," says Zipes, "for the witches and villains are no longer allegorical representations of evil in the Christian tradition but are symbolically associated with the philistine bourgeois society or the decadent aristocracy."[9]

THE BROTHERS GRIMM:
FROM FOLKLORE TO EDUCATION MANUALS

Between 1792 and 1815 the French Revolution and Napoleonic Wars devastated Europe. Territorial boundaries were continually redrawn as Napoléon usurped life, limb, and property in the name of the glory of France. Two German scholars, Jacob and Wilhelm Grimm, were deeply affected by these political events. "Despite their privileged childhood," writes professor of comparative literature Ruth Bottigheimer, "the Grimms were exposed directly to the major political traumas of the day. The French Revolution of 1789, which was followed by grisly reports of the executions of French nobles, affected Wilhelm's young imagination. His earliest extant water-color drawing depicts a bloody scene from Louis XIV's execution, as his head is held aloft before the gathered mob."[10]

Deeply concerned with the issue of German unification and imbued with the spirit of the Romantic movement that glorified the past, the Grimms pursued their nationalistic fervor by producing numerous scholarly books on German history, literature, religion, law, and folklore. This included the publication of *Kinder und Hausmärchen* (*Childhood and Household Tales*) in two volumes in 1812 and 1815, the source of many of the best-known fairy tales. Thereafter, they combined the two volumes and published another six editions. This collection of tales, including appended scholarly notes, was intended to promote German ancestral pride, not merely to be a children's book. The folkloric work of the Grimm brothers changed the attitude of scholars toward the oral tales of the people and stimulated the collecting of fairy and folktales throughout Europe. Andrew Lang's *The Blue Fairy Book* (1889), Joseph Jacobs' *English Fairy Tales* (1890), W.B. Yeats's *Fairy and Folk Tales of Ireland* (1892), and Peter Christen Asbjørnsen and Jørgen Moe's *Norwegian Folktales,* also known as *East of the Sun and West of the Moon* (1859), were among the most famous compilations of the period.

The surprising popular response to the tales, attributed to the nationalist sentiments of a growing middle-class audience, spurred Wilhelm to edit the third volume with children in mind. He described this and subsequent editions as a proper educational manual. The Grimms' tales created an ideal type for the literary fairy tale, which not only elevated the tone and style of the original folkloric texts but also made substantive thematic changes in a manner that suited the tastes of middle-class parents in Europe.

HANS CHRISTIAN ANDERSEN AND THE ART FAIRY TALE

Hans Christian Andersen's *Fairy Tales Told for Children,* published in 1835, and subsequent books of fairy tales, which included "The Little Mermaid," "The Ugly Duckling," "The Snow Queen," and "Princess and the Pea," had a profound impact on the development of the fairy tale as genre. Andersen wrote fairy tales rather than collecting or recording oral folklore. He knew and loved the Grimms' stories as a boy, but unlike the German scholars, he held no romantic notions about the glorious past of the common folk. "He knew the truth about the good old days first hand,"[11] writes biographer Frederik Bóók. His motivation came not from any nationalistic fervor but rather from an intense personal ambition to escape his lowly origins, achieve fame and recognition, and find artistic expression for his eccentric and somewhat tortured personality.

The son of a poor cobbler and illiterate washerwoman, Andersen grew up steeped in the oral tradition. As a child he invented lively tales and gave theatrical performances in his native town of Odense, Denmark. These early talents evolved into highly personal fairy tales reflecting both his hard life experience and keen powers of observation. One of Andersen's great innovations was his extraordinary imagination. His creative imaginary powers "shook the conventions of everyday existence as a lion shakes the bars of his cage,"[12] writes Böök. This changed the attitude of writers toward fantasy and fairy tales. "With the arrival of Andersen's tales in the English language," explain Iona and Peter Opie, "came an unfreezing of men's minds, an appreciation of fantasy literature and its limitless possibilities."[13] Andersen continued what Perrault had begun, writing tales that spoke with different messages to children and adults. The fairy-tale genre began to exert its influence on the imagination of writers like Charles Dickens ("The Magic Fishbone" and *A Christmas Carol*), Oscar Wilde *(The Happy Prince and Other Stories)*, Washington Irving *(Rip Van Winkle)*, and Nathaniel Hawthorne *(Tanglewood Tales for Boys and Girls)*.

THE RETURN OF THE FAIRIES TO VICTORIAN ENGLAND

As far back as English philosopher Thomas Hobbes's famous work *Leviathan*, written in 1651, the realm of fairy tales had been identified with the kingdom of darkness on English shores. Under the spell of Puritanism for the better part of two centuries, the literary establishment in England objected to fairy tales on the grounds of truth and reasonableness. In 1802 there was no greater spokesperson for the anti–fairy tale brigade than Sarah Trimmer, founder of a magazine called the *Guardian of Education*. Fearful that England and the established Christian Church were "in grave danger from the Jacobinical (or socialist) tendencies of France," she was suspect of anything of French origin, including Perrault's fairy tales. She supported the view of one anonymous magazine contributor, who wrote, "Cinderella paints some of the worst passions that can enter into the human breast, and of which little children should, if possible, be totally ignorant; such as envy, jealousy, a dislike of mothers-in-law and half-sisters, vanity, a love of dress etc etc."[14]

Major historical developments in England are said to account for the return of the credibility of fairy tales. The age of Romanticism in the late eighteenth and early nineteenth centuries heralded not only the belief in the value of the imagination and fantasy but also a more open spirit of enquiry. "The questioning spirit of the romanticists," says Zipes, "enabled them to play a key role in fostering the rise of the literary fairy tale in Great Britain, for the symbolism of the tales gave them great freedom to experiment and express their doubts about the restricted view of the utilitarians and traditional religion."[15] Robert Southey, Charles Lamb, and Samuel Coleridge pursued these questions through the fairy tales while W.B. Keats, Lord Byron, and Percy Shelley created a receptive environment for all forms of Romantic literature.

FAIRY TALES EXPRESS ALIENATION IN THE INDUSTRIAL AGE

Vast social upheaval accompanied the Industrial Revolution in the nineteenth century in Europe. The plight of the highly visible urban poor captured the attention of writers of fairy tales like John Ruskin (*King of the Golden River,* 1841), William Makepeace Thackeray (*The Rose and the Ring,* 1855) and Charles Kingsley (*The Water Babies,* 1863). These authors wrote for middle-class parents and children and looked to raise social consciousness about inequalities in English society. Charles Dickens, Lewis Caroll, and George MacDonald, the three most important writers in the genre from 1840 to 1880, wanted to develop an innovative fairy-tale form that would express the growing sense of alienation of the individual in the industrial age. They advocated change in the bureaucratic, rational, and materialist culture that had lost touch with humanity, compassion, and free-spiritedness. In Dickens', "The Magic Fishbone," he parodies a king who can only make sense of the world through reason and becomes totally confounded when his daughter, through the use of a magic fishbone, turns his world upside down and inside out. Although Carroll's *Alice's Adventures in Wonderland* serves to critique the absurd rules and regulations of his society, his use of an extraordinary plot without obvious moral purpose was a radical departure from the previous function of the genre. MacDonald's "The Light Princess," which parodies "Sleeping Beauty," tells of a princess who is cursed with a lack of gravity following an insult to a fairy godmother. When she sees a noble prince about to die because of her frivolity, she is transformed through compassion into a mature human being and gains the gravity necessary for good human relations.

Between 1860 and the turn of the century, fairy-tale writers moved in one of two directions. The first, represented by authors like Italian Carlo Collodi, who wrote *Pinocchio* in 1883, aimed to instill solid values like diligence and perseverance in the very young and uphold established norms. Writers who chose the other path, like Oscar Wilde, Kenneth Graham, Rudyard Kipling, and Robert Louis Stevenson, sought to reform the conventional fairy tale to expose readers to new views on authority, socialization, religion, and gender roles. They were joined by a number of female fairy-tale writers, including Christina Rosetti, Anne Thackeray Ritchie, and Frances Hodgson Burnett, who expressed radical, angry, even violent views under the guise of the innocent fairy tale. Zipes concludes, "These writers instilled a Utopian spirit into the fairy tale discourse that endowed the genre with a vigorous and unique quality of social criticism, which was to be developed even further by later writers of faerie works such as A.A. Milne, J.R.R. Tolkien, C.S. Lewis and T.H. White."[16]

AMERICAN FAIRY TALES AND IDEALISM

In an effort to explain the paucity of early American authors who wrote fairy tales, American writer and critic Selma G. Lanes asserts that the traditional fairy tale was "out of tune with the freshly minted optimism generated by the New World" in nineteenth-century America. "Fairy Tales were consolations for lives in need of magical solutions, but here man was master of his own fate."[17]

Washington Irving's *Rip Van Winkle*, written in 1819, is considered the first serious attempt to adapt the European fairy tale to American soil. It took more than half a century for other American contenders to weigh in. Frank R. Stockton, hailed as the pioneer of American fairy tales, published *The Bee Man of Orn and Other Fanciful Tales* in 1887. Representative of a new breed of fairy-tale writers, Stockton and his contemporaries were drawn to the genre to express their views on the greed and materialism of the Gilded Age in America. Stockton's fairy tales convey his concerns about abuses of authority and offer a social vision that stresses inner contentment. In 1900 L. Frank Baum, who set out to write a distinctly American fairy tale, published *The Wonderful Wizard of Oz*. In a sequel, Princess Langwidere asks Dorothy, "Are you of royal blood?" Emphasizing America's detachment from European aristocracy and anything that smacked of the Old World, Dorothy pluckily replies, "Better than that, ma'am, I come from Kansas."[18] Baum consciously departed from the Grimm/Andersen fairy-tale model in response to what British writer and critic Neil Phillip describes as a growing sense that European fairy tales were "failing American children in some deep-seated way."[19]

The American fairy tale differed from its European counterpart in several important respects. A certain idealism penetrated the genre and showed itself in different values, in a new conception of the use of magic, and in the nature of the relationship between good and evil. The heroes and heroines in American fairy tales sought courage, heart, and adventure rather than riches, power, and status. Magic was secondary to the overriding reality of American life experience. In Stockton's "The Bee Man of Orn," for example, after many adventures, the hero returns to his normal everyday life and sees it with fresh appreciation. Similarly, much of the power of the traditional European fairy tales came from the evenly matched forces of good and evil. But in the American versions, the wolf does not get Red Riding Hood, and Dorothy in Baum's Oz tales is not harmed because the power of good is always portrayed as greater than the power of evil. In the words of Lanes, early American writers of fairy tales had a "reluctance to give wickedness its due."[20] This rosy picture of American life and human nature became unglued in the twentieth century, when writers of fairy tales witnessed the world wars, the Great Depression, the Cold War, and disturbing developments in America's social fabric.

THE POLITICIZATION OF THE GENRE IN THE TWENTIETH CENTURY

By the twentieth century the literary fairy tale was fully institutionalized and commanded a major role in forming and maintaining the cultural heritage of Western society. This meant that publishing houses regularly produced books of fairy tales to meet an established demand by consumers. Fairy-tale themes and stories proliferated in a range of art forms, including music, opera, plays, poetry, the visual arts, and, more recently, film and television. Folklorist Wolfgang Mieder attests to the recent upsurge in innovative fairy-tale forms to include cartoons, comic strips, newspaper headlines, and advertisements. Creators of these art forms draw on the near-universal language of fairy tales but shape them to impress specific social and political visions on their work.

Politicization was a marked feature of the genre during the first half of the twentieth century. The devastation caused by World War I prompted a number of writers to express political views through fairy-tale forms. For example, in 1919 Hermann Hesse gave his pacifist views in "Strange News from Another Planet." Thomas Mann produced his fairy-tale novel *The Magic Mountain* (1924), which was full of covert ideological messages, and, according to Jack Zipes, J.R.R. Tolkien's *The Hobbit* (1938) was written as a warning tale about the dangers of a second world war.

In the late 1930s the Nazis rise to power in Europe saw evidence of a more sinister use of the genre. The German Pedagogical Academy published Nazi interpretations of the Grimms' fairy tales, including a version of "Cinderella" in which the prince recognizes Cinderella's purity of blood while ensuring that her racially inferior stepmother and stepsisters receive their just desserts. The blatant use of the genre for indoctrination purposes continued into the Cold War era. In East Germany, Marxist versions of fairy tales such as "Cinderella" were altered to reflect the rejection by the prince of his former "parasitic existence" within the royal family and the palace and his subsequent preference for joining Cinderella as one of the common folk.

THE "DISNEYFICATION" OF AMERICA

While writers in Europe carried on their own experiments with fairy tales, a significant innovation took place in America that would have tremendous influence on the genre. In an effort to uplift sagging morale and encourage workers to pull together during the Great Depression, Walt Disney released the classic film *Snow White and the Seven Dwarfs* in 1937. This animated film, along with Disney's *Cinderella*, broke all box-office records. The film medium and the enormous appeal of his animated characters ensured that Disney's versions would be seen by millions of people worldwide. So influential were his fairy-tale features that they often supplanted the original tales on which they were based. A report from *Newsweek* in 1973 maintains that at the time of his death in 1966, Disney had entertained and educated three generations of Americans. Disney's fairy tales continue to play a role in uniting parents, children, and

people of different walks of life in the pleasures of enchantment and in providing a distraction from some of the
harsher realities of the late twentieth century.

However, the vast commercialization of the genre with
Disney theme parks, movies, videos, and toys has fueled a
heated critical debate concerning Disney's treatment of the
fairy tale as genre and his impact on the socialization
process. In placing his main focus on technical innovations,
critics claim that Disney has trivialized and sanitized the
genuine tales beyond all recognition. For example, the authentic Cinderella tale is not one of rags to riches, a heroine
dreaming of being rescued by a prince. In the tale derived
from the oral tradition, Cinderella is a princess who has had
a spell cast on her that hides her true identity and forces her
to be a lowly housemaid. With the help of the spirit of her
dead mother, she meets the conditions to have the wicked
spell released when she is recognized and loved by a prince
for her true beauty and inner nobility of spirit despite her
filthy outward appearance. "With Mr. Disney's treatment,"
said American librarian Frances Clarke-Sayers in a famous
letter to the *Los Angeles Times* in 1965, "the powerful ancient
tales fraught with psychological conflict and spiritual truths
become one great marshmallow-covered cream puff."[21]

Similarly, feminist critics argue that Disney's heroines
provide poor female role models. Speaking of Snow White
and Cinderella, Marina Warner says Disney portrays
"niminy-piminy idiots as paragons and introduce children
everywhere to expect malignancy from older women."[22]
Marcia Lieberman, in her acclaimed article " 'Some Day My
Prince Will Come': Female Acculturation Through the Fairy
Tale," says fairy tales are "training manuals in passive behavior"[23] for women. However, other feminist writers such
as professor of American literature Alison Lurie point to the
sterling qualities of heroines in earlier oral tales and suggest
their emancipatory nature. More recent feminist scholars,
including Madonna Kolbenschlag and Kay Stone, believe
classical fairy tales can be both "parables of socialization"[24]
for women and at the same time models for radical transformation of their lives.

Despite the views of feminists, academics, and educators,
the popular appeal of the Disney fairy tales remained a major cultural influence and a reflection of values in the late
twentieth century. For example, critics claim that they both

reflect and perpetuate sexual stereotypes that have promoted passivity in women and placed pressure on men to fulfill certain role expectations. "Disney's modifications originate from accurate readings of our culture," says American writer and librarian Betsy Hearne. "He got the address right. This is where we live. We who criticize Disney have seen the enemy, and he is us. . . . What he does to fairy tales and classics is, in a sense, our own shadow. We don't have to like it and we don't have to keep quiet about it, but we do have to understand our own society and the lore it generates."[25]

In response to feminist concerns over Disney's sanitized variants and a predominance of fairy tales with passive heroines, writers cast a critical eye on the genre and explored new avenues of female empowerment in the classic tales. Rosemary Minard scanned folklore texts for pithy females and published *Womenfolk and Fairy Tales* in 1975. Pamela Travers, in *About the Sleeping Beauty,* collected multiple versions of the fairy tale from around the world and included her own updated version, suggesting that the awakening of Sleeping Beauty is symbolic of an awakening of the soul that has somehow fallen asleep after childhood and has become hemmed in and hidden by the external affairs of life. Authors such as Anne Sexton, Jane Yolen, Tanith Lee, Angela Carter, and Terri Windling have rewritten the old tales and created bold texts presenting a new breed of fairy-tale heroines as models for women. In Judith Viorst's Cinderella tale, for example, the heroine changes her mind when she sees the prince in the cold light of day and pretends the slipper does not fit.

FAIRY TALES ADDRESS MODERN SOCIAL CONCERNS

Like the feminist critics, other modern writers have continued to use fairy tales as vehicles of social commentary. Struck by the incongruence between the idealism of these classic tales and the harsh realities of the modern world, these writers chose to explore a more pessimistic anti–fairy-tale philosophy. Sarah Moon's *Little Red Riding Hood* uses Perrault's text with her own stark modern photography to present a disturbing commentary on modern social tragedies. A young girl sets out for her grandmother's house only to be raped and beaten in city streets on the way. And in the late 1980s, Ron Koslow's television series *Beauty and the Beast* presented a typical New York yuppie lawyer involved with a successful real estate developer, who has her shallow life turned upside down after being raped in Central Park. Found close to death by a beastlike creature who inhabits an underground world, she is nursed back to health. In the process, she develops a social conscience, is "humanized" by the beast, and becomes a legal champion for the downtrodden.

Innovative uses of the genre have also included drawing on the powerful metaphors and symbolism to illuminate people's psychological conflicts. In his classic work *The Uses of Enchantment: The Meaning and Importance of Fairy Tales,* Freudian child psychiatrist Bruno Bettelheim suggests that many popular fairy tales symbolically depict emotional anxieties and can be used to help troubled children develop a sense of meaning in their lives. Following Bettelheim's work, psychology professor Sheldon Cashdan has drawn on the tale of "Cinderella" to illustrate the pitfalls of envy; "Jack and the Beanstalk," greed; "Hansel and Gretel," gluttony; and "Snow White," vanity, in his use of the genre to treat disturbed children.

AGGRESSIVE AND DISTURBING POSTMODERNIST FAIRY TALES

In the last decades of the twentieth century, the genre showed more aggressive tendencies. Through the use of highly disturbing fairy-tale images and dark departures from happy endings, artists like Emma Donoghue, Wendy Walker, and Robert Coover created highly experimental fairy-tale forms. These have been designed to shock people out of complacency and have left audiences unsettled and dissatisfied. Coover's "Hansel and Gretel" is a good example. The modernized Hansel and Gretel arrive at the witch's house, which is dark and frightening and greatly contrasts with the bright gingerbread house of the old tale. The tale concludes, "But the door: here they pause and catch their breath. It is heart-shaped and blood-stone-red, its burnished surface gleaming in the sunlight. Oh, what a thing is that door! Shining like a ruby, like hard cherry candy, and pulsing softly, radiantly. Yes, marvelous! insuperable! but beyond: what is that sound of black rags flapping?"[26] The traditional triumphant ending to the tale is bypassed, leaving the reader anxious but with no clear resolution. The primary function of the fairy tale—to provide hope and closure—has been undermined. According to Jack Zipes, the object of these postmodernist fairy-tale writers is to jolt the reader into new awareness, to question old assumptions with an alert and critical eye, and "to hold a cracked mirror to the old fairy tales and reality at the same time."[27]

Zipes suggests that the directions the genre will take in the future include the continued reproduction of classical tales for children, at the forefront of which is still the Disney animated verisons; feminist fairy tales designed to express concerns about women's roles in the twenty-first century; postmodern experimental forms with unusual twists like Coover's rendition of "Hansel and Gretel"; and parodies and revisions of the classical tales in a variety of forms, including commercials, films, and literature, both to amuse and to question convention. Sheldon Cashdan predicts that in the future the genre will be wedded to computer technology, which may lead to fairy tales in the world of virtual reality. Here, a young child might become Jack, scrambling down the beanstalk, or scale a castle wall to wake a sleeping princess. The classical tales would be given new dimensions as children experience fairy-tale characters and worlds from the inside out.

THE SIGNIFICANCE OF THE GENRE

One is struck by the antiquity of the fairy tale and by the variety of functions it has served during its long history. From civilizing, to subverting, to indoctrinating, to shocking audiences out of old beliefs, to molding new social patterns, fairy tales interact with societies and emerge in new forms. They reflect the values and concerns of the storyteller, the audience, and the times. Yet although their shapes and forms change, core elements endure. Cinderella is alive and well, whatever her modern-day apparel, an eternal fairy-tale heroine.

What can account for the longevity and tenacity of the genre? Why are the tales so compelling? Classical fairy tales mirror the process of growth, transformation, and maturity. American author Joseph Campbell says fairy tales present the archetype for the hero's journey. The initiate is cast out of the old and familiar, is alienated and lost, faces terrible danger, wins a great victory, and emerges from this mysterious journey with the power to bestow knowledge and wisdom on his fellow man. Campbell suggests that the longevity of the genre is related to its eternal relevance to human history.

The compelling nature of fairy tales is partly related to their unique style and effect. Fairy tales contain magical occurrences that astonish and enchant. The world beyond "once upon a time" is a place free of ancient limitations like poverty, hunger, and death, and where deep soul longings, like flying as free as the birds or talking to the beasts, can find expression. In the fairy-tale form, writers like C.S. Lewis have seen the opportunity to "bypass the watchful dragons"[28] of the rational mind and present ideas to people that they would normally not admit. Tolkien says the effect of fairy tales is not amenable to rational analysis. Fairy tales open a door on "other time," which is free from strict adherence to rational laws and concepts.

Tolkien further maintains that the consolation of the happy ending, an essential characteristic of all true fairy tales, is the highest and most primary function of the genre. Classic fairy tales do not deny the existence of heartache and sorrow, but they do deny universal defeat. And, according to Tolkien, fairy tales produce a special kind of joy, "joy beyond the walls, poignant as grief,"[29] as keen as that produced by any literary art form. The joy elicited by fairy tales, however, can pass outside the web of story, or make-believe, and provide a glimpse of an underlying truth or reality. Fairy tales are so compelling because they arouse an intuitive knowing that there is a profound truth in the vicinity. It is a highly subjective call, and again, not open to rational analysis. Roger Sale gives an example of this as he describes his reaction to the final lines of the Grimms' tale "The Death of the Hen," which read, "So the cock was left all alone with the dead hen, and he digged a grave and laid her in it, and he raised a mound above her, and sat himself down and lamented so sore that at last he died. And they were all dead together." Sale's epiphany is unrestrained:

> I feel here almost like shouting. There is nothing like this in the world, never before and never again. . . . We are back at the foot of the great narrative tree, where stories can, as if by a kind of natural magic, go anywhere, because life, crimped and fearful though it be, is wondrous and full and one must accept it all. One minds mortality less when remembering that we will all be dead together, along with the hen and the cock and the teller of that tale.[30]

The wonder and recognition of the profound nature of something so deceptively innocent lures readers like Sale back to the genre, back to the magic and enchantment of the fairy-tale realm.

NOTES

1. Roger Sale, *Fairy Tales and After: From Snow White to E.B. White.* Cambridge, MA: Harvard University Press, 1978, p. 26.

2. Quoted in Rosan A. Jordon and Susan J. Kalcik, eds., *Women's Folklore, Women's Culture.* Philadelphia: University of Pennsylvania Press, 1985, p. 131.

3. Jack Zipes, *When Dreams Came True: Classical Fairy Tales and Their Tradition.* New York: Routledge, 1999, p. 1.

4. J.R.R. Tolkien, *Tree and Leaf.* Boston: Houghton Mifflin, 1965, p. 6.

5. Zipes, *When Dreams Came True,* p. 8.

6. Zipes, *When Dreams Came True,* pp. 13–14.

7. Zipes, *When Dreams Came True,* p. 40.

8. Charles Perrault, *Memoirs of My Life.* Columbia: University of Missouri Press, 1989, p. 18.

9. Zipes, *When Dreams Came True,* p. 18.

10. Ruth Bottigheimer, *Grimms' Bad Girls and Bold Boys: The Moral and Social Vision of the Tales.* New Haven, CT: Yale University Press, 1987, p. 3.

11. Frederik Böök, *Hans Christian Andersen: A Biography.* Norman: University of Oklahoma Press, 1963, p. 216.

12. Böök, *Hans Christian Andersen,* p. 207.

13. Iona and Peter Opie, *The Classic Fairy Tales.* London: Oxford University Press, 1974, p. 34.

14. Quoted in F.J. Harvey Darton, *Children's Books in England: Five Centuries of Social Life.* London: Cambridge University Press, 1966, pp. 96–97.

15. Zipes, *When Dreams Came True,* p. 113.

16. Zipes, *When Dreams Came True,* p. 127.

17. Selma G. Lanes, *Down the Rabbit Hole: Adventures and Misadventures in the Realm of Children's Literature.* New York: Atheneum, 1971, p. 92.

18. Quoted in Neil Phillip, *American Fairy Tales.* New York: Hyperion, 1996, p. 153.

19. Phillip, *American Fairy Tales,* p. 154.

20. Lanes, *Down the Rabbit Hole,* p. 104.

21. Frances Clarke-Sayers, "Walt Disney Accused," *Horn Book Magazine,* December 1965, p. 602.

22. Marina Warner, "Beauty and the Beasts," *Sight and Sound,* 6, 1992, p. 11.

23. Marcia Lieberman, " 'Some Day My Prince Will Come': Female Acculturation Through the Fairy Tale," *College English,* 1972, p. 383.

24. Madonna Kolbenschlag, *Kiss Sleeping Beauty Good-Bye: Breaking the Spell of Feminine Myths and Models.* Toronto: Bantam, 1981, p. 3.

25. Betsy Hearne, "Disney Revisited, or, Jiminy Cricket, It's Musty Down Here," *Horn Book Magazine,* March/April 1997, pp. 137–47.

26. Quoted in Jack Zipes, *Fairy Tale as Myth/Myth as Fairy Tale.* Lexington: University Press of Kentucky, 1994, pp. 158–59.

27. Zipes, *Fairy Tale as Myth,* p. 159.

28. C.S. Lewis, *Of Other Worlds: Essays and Stories.* New York: Harcourt Brace, 1967, p. 37.

29. Tolkien, *Tree and Leaf,* p. 68.

30. Sale, *Fairy Tales and After,* pp. 46–47.

CHAPTER 1

Characteristics of the Genre

Fairy Tales

Defining Fairy Tales

Marcia Lane

Marcia Lane is known for her fairy tale storytelling concert performances in the United States and Europe. Creator of the AMTRAK Storytelling Odyssey, she traveled to thirty-nine communities across America telling stories and riding the rails. Lane wrote *Picturing the Rose, A Way of Looking at Fairy Tales* to help the beginning or accomplished storyteller grasp the nature and meaning of the ancient tales, and provide practical tips for their performance. At that time, she was Assistant Director of Education at Carnegie Hall in New York. In the following extract she explains the difference between myths, legends, folk tales, and fairy tales. Though experts don't agree on a precise definition for a fairy tale, major elements include the feeling or sensation of the mysterious, a supernatural setting, the presence of a magical being, the use of the past tense but with no mention of specifics, and the classic opening lines, "Once upon a time."

Do you remember the first fairy tale you ever heard? Probably not. The very first fairy tale you ever heard probably went into your brain, rattled around for a while, disrupted a few neurons, and departed. But it left its mark on your ability to perceive certain implications about time and space and gender and many other facets of life and language.

In time you heard many other fairy tales. Some you liked and asked for over and over again, and some you hated on first hearing! Some were promptly dismissed. But with each additional tale, you gained a certain level of understanding of these issues: real versus symbolic, here versus somewhere, possible versus "im-". We form a picture of inner and outer life through an understanding, not only of the stories we are hearing, but also which types of stories.

A Difficult Genre to Define

With the exception of literary fairy tales (a genre that has only really been recognized since the stories of the early nineteenth century), all orally transmitted fairy tales are folktales, but not all folktales are fairy tales. By that I mean that all of those stories come from an oral tradition, but not all satisfy the requirements—anybody's requirements—for fairy tales. The exact definition of "fairy tale" has been a matter of debate for a long time. Even the "experts" agree that, for a story to qualify as a traditional fairy tale, it must contain certain elements, but they don't all agree on what those elements are. There may be a supernatural or magical being, a sort of "fairy substitute," if you will! Therefore, stories with genies, ogres, imps, wizards, brownies, witches, sorcerers, oni, or fairies are all fairy tales. Beyond that stipulation, however, it all falls apart. Some writers on the subject firmly believe that if there is no supernatural being, then there is no fairy tale. Others feel that any magical occurrence fills the bill. You might say that a talking animal is a magical creature, but in many common European folktales (and in Native American and African stories) the animals talk up a storm, and the effect is one of ordinariness, not magic. Perhaps it is safe to say that a talking animal is only remarkable when the story chooses to remark on it. "The King, however, had a lion which was a wondrous animal, for he knew all concealed and secret things." So, in the Grimms' fairy tale "The Twelve Huntsmen," the story itself tells us that the lion is magical, not because he can speak, but because he has a special vision. He can see the truth.

The Enchanted Realm

In his classic work "On Fairy-Stories", fantasy writer J.R.R. Tolkien says fairy tales are not only stories about elves and fairies, but rather stories about "Faërie", which is a magical realm where fairies and all manner of marvels reside.

Faërie contains many things besides elves and fays, and besides dwarfs, witches, trolls, giants, or dragons: it holds the seas, the sun, the moon, the sky; and the earth, and all things that are in it: tree and bird, water and stone, wine and bread, and ourselves, mortal men, when we are enchanted.

J.R.R. Tolkien, *Tree and Leaf*, 1965.

ISSUES OF TIME, PLACE, AND NARRATIVE VOICE

There are other issues involved in classifying fairy tales. It is generally accepted that if a story is represented as having happened to a real person (living or dead) then it qualifies as a legend—no matter how magical the events in the story. Likewise, if a story happens at a particular time (that is, "in 1492," for example) then it may be history or legend or lie, but it is usually not fairy tale. Issues of time may, indeed, be magical. In the classic Japanese fairy tale "Urashima" the hero spends three nights under the sea, and when he returns to land he finds that three hundred years have passed. The Washington Irving story "Rip Van Winkle" employs the same device, but in this case we know the author, so folklorists and storytellers generally regard this as a literary legend, and not one from the oral tradition. That holds true even though Irving may have used many of the local Catskill traditional oral legends in the body of the story.

Another measure of oral story versus literary is the presence of a distinctive "author's voice." This is, at one end of the spectrum, fairly obvious. For example, it's obvious that the language in "Rip Van Winkle" is the creation of a specific nineteenth-century author, and therefore not characteristic of a fairy tale. It is highly stylized, and not a product of the oral tradition. "In the High and Far-Off Times the Elephant, O Best Beloved, ... ," is an opening phrase that marks a story as one of Rudyard Kipling's *Just So Stories*. On the other hand, there are gifted story-writers who choose to hide (or, at least, soften) the evidence of single authorship. Jane Yolen, Richard Kennedy, Eleanor Farjeon, and Alan Garner are just a few examples of contemporary writers whose works have a timeless, classic feel to them.

The task of making hard and fast decisions about what is or is not a fairy tale has become more difficult and complex as the lines between oral and literary have blurred. Most of the literary stories of seventeenth-century author Charles Perrault were oral fairy tales before he wrote them down, and are definitely considered "classic" fairy tales now. But C. Perrault is still in the picture! After all, like the Grimm brothers, Perrault did write, and by writing, codify those stories that we modern tellers adapt, adopt, and tell. He also edited, arranged, and selected the stories. All in all, it is getting harder and harder to separate the folk from the author in most story collections that purport to be "pure."

Even in cases where there are no magical occurrences, no chatty animals, no ogres, there may still be a fairy tale! The story that happens in a place that is more of the mind than of the map—that is a fairy tale. In *Hard Facts of the Grimms' Fairy Tales* (1987), Maria Tatar [Professor of German Literature at Harvard University] describes a continuum from folklore (oral literature) to literature (the written-down variety). Then she plots an intersecting line that runs between naturalistic and supernaturalistic settings. Tatar describes fairy tales as stories that occur in supernatural settings, and may be either oral or written literature. Folktales are defined as those stories that happen in naturalistic settings and, again, may be either oral or written. According to Tatar, the Grimms' stories fall into all four quadrants, depending on

Naturalistic Setting	
Oral Folktales	Literary Folktales
Jack and the King's Daughter (U.S.)	When Schlemeil Went to Warsaw (L.B. Singer)
The Boy Who Went to the North Wind (Norway)	The Rootabaga Stories (Carl Sandburg)
How Frog Got Long Legs (Ghana)	
Folklore	Literature
Oral Fairy Tales	Literary Fairy Tales
Rapunzel	The Girl Who Cried Flowers (Yolen)
The Twelve Huntsmen	The Caliph Stork (Hauptmann)
Urashima	The Water of Life (Pyle)
Supernaturalistic Setting	

Note: Based on a diagram by Maria Tatar with story titles added by Marcia Lane

the nature of the story, and on how much creative rewriting was done between the original source and the published version.

If you think about the opening "lines" of a story, any story, you can see that genre usually reveals itself in the first moments of the telling. "In the beginning . . ." —no matter what is said after that moment, this story has marked itself as a myth. Other traditional "myth-markers" would be "Once, in the beginning of days . . ." or "Before people were made . . . ." Personal stories refer to the teller, as in, "When my father was ten, he got his first pet, a pug dog." Obviously, no matter how much rewriting has gone into this tale, it comes from a particular perspective, a personal historical reference. "There was once a farmer and his wife, and they were forever arguing about who had the harder job." There, in one sentence, is a folktale! Now, if the story goes on to describe a test of wills, silly accidents, reconciliation, then it is a common, garden-variety folktale. If, however, an imp comes out of the sugar bowl and creates havoc, or if the husband catches a golden fish that begs for its life, then you have a fairy tale.

FAIRY TALES VERSUS MYTHS, LEGENDS, AND FANTASY

My own definition of fairy tale goes something like this: A fairy tale is a story—literary or folk—that has a sense of the numinous, the feeling or sensation of the supernatural or the mysterious. But, and this is crucial, it is a story that happens in the past tense, and a story that is not tied to any specifics. If it happens "at the beginning of the world," then it is a myth. A story that names a specific "real" person is a legend (even if it contains a magical occurrence). A story that happens in the future is a fantasy. Fairy tales are sometimes spiritual, but never religious.

It may be cold comfort to the novice teller, but the truth is that after reading and telling dozens of stories you will find that a true fairy tale, like gold, tends to make its presence felt. And, like class, although undefinable, everyone knows it when they see it!

Studying the Fairy Tale

Alan Dundes

There is no ambiguity among folklorists over how to
define a fairy tale. Through careful analysis of oral
folktales, a special sub group of stories with specific
plot lines has been designated 'tales of magic.' In the
following article, Alan Dundes, professor of Anthro-
pology and Folklore at the University of California,
Berkeley, points out some of the errors researchers
make in claiming to study fairy tales. He says that all
literary renditions, even those like the Grimm brothers' tales which claim to be authentic recordings of
oral tales, have been altered by collectors to serve
their own ends. Fairy tales are to be heard, not read.
Dundes does not dismiss the usefulness of written
tales, but he stresses that they should be studied as
variants of the original oral forms. He also notes the
Indo-European bias that exists in the classification of
the genre, which excludes tales found amongst indigenous groups in North and South America, Africa,
and aboriginal Australia. Dundes has written extensively on fairy tales and has edited casebooks on
"Cinderella" and "Little Red Riding Hood."

The first thing to say about fairy tales is that they are an oral
form. Fairy tales, however one may choose ultimately to define them, are a subgenre of the more inclusive category of
"folktale," which exists primarily as a spoken traditional
narrative. Once a fairy tale or any other type of folktale, for
that matter, is reduced to written language, one does not
have a true fairy tale but instead only a pale and inadequate
reflection of what was originally an oral performance complete with raconteur and audience. From this folkloristic
perspective, one cannot possibly read fairy tales; one can
only properly hear them told.

Excerpted from "Fairy Tales from a Folklorist Perspective," by Alan Dundes in *Fairy
Tales and Society: Illusion, Allusion, and Paradigm*, edited by Ruth Bottigheimer. Copy-
right © 1986 by University of Pennsylvania Press. Reprinted with permission from the
University of Pennsylvania Press.

When one enters into the realm of written-down or transcribed fairy tales, one is involved with a separate order of reality. A vast chasm separates an oral tale with its subtle nuances entailing significant body movements, eye expression, pregnant pauses, and the like from the inevitably flat and fixed written record of what was once a live and often compelling storytelling event. To be sure, there are degrees of authenticity and accuracy with respect to the transcription of fairy tales. In modern times, armed with tape recorders or videotape equipment, a folklorist may be able to capture a live performance in the act, thereby preserving it for enjoyment and study by future audiences. But in the nineteenth century when the formal study of folklore began in Europe, collectors had to do the best they could to take down oral tales verbatim without such advances in technology. Many of them succeeded admirably, such as E. Tang Kristensen (1843–1929), a Danish folklorist who was one of the greatest collectors of fairy tales of all time. Others, including even the celebrated Grimm brothers, failed to live up to the ideal of recording oral tales as they were told. Instead, they altered the oral tales in a misguided effort to "improve" them. The Grimms, for instance, began to conflate different versions of the same tale and they ended up producing what folklorists now call "composite" texts. A composite text, containing one motif from one version, another motif from another, and so on, exemplifies what folklorists term "fakelore." Fakelore refers to an item which the collector claims is genuine oral tradition but which has been doctored or in some cases entirely fabricated by the purported collector.

The point is that a composite fairy tale has never actually been told in precisely that form by a storyteller operating in the context of oral tradition. It typically appears for the very first time in print. And it is not just a matter of twentieth-century scholars trying to impose twentieth-century standards upon struggling nineteenth-century pioneering collectors. For the Grimms certainly knew better, and they are on record as adamantly opposing the literary reworking of folklore (as had been done in the famous folksong anthology of *Des Knaben Wunderhorn* [1805] which they severely criticized). They specifically called for the collection of fairy tales as they were told—in dialect. In the preface to the first volume of the *Kinder- und Hausmärchen* [Childhood and

Household Tales] of 1812, the Grimms bothered to say that they had "endeavored to present these fairy tales as pure as possible. . . . No circumstance has been added, embellished or changed." Unfortunately, they were later unable or unwilling to adhere to these exemplary criteria. So the Grimms knew what they were doing when they combined different versions of a single folktale and presented it as one of the tales in their *Kinder- und Hausmärchen.*

LITERARY BIAS IN STUDY OF FAIRY TALES

What this means is that anyone truly interested in the unadulterated fairy tale must study oral texts or as accurate a transcription of oral texts as is humanly possible. The reality of far too much of what passes for fairy tale scholarship . . . is that such fairy tale texts are not considered. Instead, a strong, elitist literary bias prevails and it is the recast and reconstituted fairy tales which serve as the corpus for study. When one analyzes fairy tales as rewritten by Charles Perrault or by the Grimm brothers, one is *not* analyzing fairy tales as they were told by traditional storytellers. One is instead analyzing fairy tale plots as altered by men of letters, often with a nationalistic and romantic axe to grind. The aim was usually to present evidence of an ancient nationalistic patrimony in which the French or German literati could take pride. With such a laudable goal, it was deemed excusable to eliminate any crude or vulgar elements—How many bawdy folktales does one find in the Grimm canon?—and to polish and refine the oral discourse of "rough" peasant dialects.

This does not mean that versions, composite or not, of tales published by Perrault and the Grimms cannot be studied. They have had an undeniably enormous impact upon popular culture and literature, but they should not be confused with the genuine article—the oral fairy tale.

There is another difficulty with the research carried out by deluded individuals who erroneously believe they are studying fairy tales when they limit themselves to the Grimm or Perrault versions of tales. Any true fairy tale, like all folklore, is characterized by the criteria of "multiple existence" and "variation." An item must exist in at least two versions in order to qualify as authentic folklore. Most items exist in hundreds of versions. Usually, no two versions of an oral fairy tale will be exactly word-for-word the same. That is what is meant by the criteria of multiple existence and variation. When one studies the Perrault or the Grimm text of a fairy tale, one is studying a single text. This may be appropriate for literary scholars who are wont to think in terms of unique, distinctive, individual texts written by a known author or poet. But it is totally inappropriate for the study of folklore wherein there is no such thing as *the* text. There are only texts.

CLASSIFICATION OF FOLK AND FAIRY TALES

Folklorists have been collecting fairy tales and other forms of folklore for the past several centuries. Not all these versions have been published. In fact, the majority of these tales remain in unpublished form scattered in folklore archives throughout the world. However, one can obtain these versions simply by applying to these archives. Folklorists have carried out extensive comparative studies of various fairy tales in which they have assiduously located and assembled as many as five hundred versions of a single tale type. Ever since the Finnish folklorist Antti Aarne published his *Verzeichnis der Märchentypen* . . . in 1910, folklorists have had an index of folktales (including fairy tales). Twice revised by American folklorist Stith Thompson, in 1928 and again in 1961, *The Types of the Folktale: A Classification and Bibliography*, is the standard reference for any serious student of Indo-European folktales. Thompson's revisions took account of the various local, regional, and national tale type indexes which appeared after Aarne's 1910 work. There are more than fifty or sixty national tale-type indexes in print, including several which are not referenced in the Aarne-Thompson 1961 index inasmuch as they were published after that date, for example for Latvia, China, Korea, Madagascar, Friesland, and Norway.

The Aarne-Thompson tale-type index gives not only a general synopsis of each of some two thousand Indo-European tales, but also some sense of how many versions are to be found in the various folklore archives. In addition, if there is a published article or monograph which contains numerous versions of a tale type, it is listed followed by an asterisk. If there has been a substantial, full-fledged comparative study of a particular tale, that bibliographical citation is marked by two asterisks. Thus if one looked in the Aarne-Thompson tale-type index under tale type 425A, "The Monster (Animal) as Bridegroom (Cupid and Psyche)," one would in a matter of seconds discover no less than five double-asterisked monographs or articles devoted to this tale type. One would also learn that there are eighty-seven Danish versions, twenty-eight Hungarian versions, twenty-nine Rumanian versions, and others located in archives.

The gist of this is that if one is really interested in a particular fairy tale, one has the possibility of considering dozens upon dozens of versions of that tale. Whatever one's particular theoretical interest, the comparative data is essential. If one is concerned with identifying possible national traits in a particular version of a tale, one cannot do so without first ascertaining whether the traits in question are found in versions of the same tale told in other countries. If the same traits are to be found in twenty countries, it would be folly to assume that those traits were somehow typical of German or French culture exclusively.

FALSE GENERALIZATIONS BASED ON A SINGLE VERSION

The sad truth is that most studies of fairy tales are carried out in total ignorance of tale-type indexes (or the related tool, the six volume *Motif-Index of Folk Literature* which first appeared in 1932–36, and was revised in 1955–58). One can say categorically that it is always risky, methodologically speaking, *to limit one's analysis to one single version of a tale.* There is absolutely no need to restrict one's attention to a single version of a tale type when there are literally hundreds of versions of that same tale easily available. The fallacy of using but a single version of a fairy tale is compounded when that one version is a doctored, rewritten composite text, as occurs when one uses the Grimm version alone. . . .

It is hard to document the extent of the parochialism of the bulk of fairy-tale research. There are too few folklorists and too many amateurs. For example, one continues to find essays and books naively claiming to extrapolate German national or cultural traits from the Grimm tales. It is not that there could not be any useful data contained in the Grimm versions, it is rather that there are plenty of authentic versions of German fairy tales available which a would-be student of German culture could consult as a check. Psychiatrists writing about fairy tales commit the same error. They typically use only one version of a fairy tale, in most instances the Grimm version, and then they go on to generalize not just about German culture, but all European culture or even all humankind—on the basis of one single (rewritten) version of a fairy tale. This displays a certain arrogance, ethnocentrism, and ignorance.

INDO-EUROPEAN BIAS IN FAIRY TALE CLASSIFICATION

There is another important question with respect to fairy tales. If one were to read through symposia and books devoted to the fairy tale . . . one could easily come to the (false) conclusion that the fairy tale, strictly speaking, was a European form. Certainly, if one speaks only of Perrault and the Grimms, one is severely restricted—just to France and Germany, not even considering the fairy tale traditions of Eastern Europe. But is the fairy tale a subgenre of folktale limited in distribution to Europe or to the Indo-European (and Semitic) world? Are there fairy tales in Africa? in Polynesia? among North and South American Indians? If one defines fairy tales as consisting of Aarne-Thompson tale types 300 to 749, the so-called tales of magic—as opposed let us say to animal tales (Aarne-Thompson tale types 1–299) or numskull stories (AT 1200–1349) . . . then one would have a relatively closed corpus. [Russian Folklorist] Vladimir Propp, for example, in his pioneering *Morphology of the Folktale*, first published in 1928, tried to define the structure of the "fairy tale," that is, Aarne-Thompson tale types 300–749. The Swedish folklore theorist C. W. von Sydow proposed the term *chimerate*, [from chimera, meaning fanciful conception] which included AT 300–749 *and* AT 850–879, which is perhaps a better sampling of the so-called European fairy tale.

The point is that these Aarne-Thompson tale types are *not* universal. They are basically Indo-European (plus Semitic, Chinese, and so on) tale types. "Cinderella," for example, AT 510A although extremely widespread in the Indo-European world is not found as an indigenous tale in North and South America, in Africa, or aboriginal Australia. In other words, more than half the peoples of the world do not have a version of "Cinderella" except as borrowed from Indo-European cultures. But they have their own tales. The question is: Are some of their tales fairy tales? Is the tale of Star-Husband which is found throughout native North America a "fairy tale"? An abundant scholarship has been devoted to this American Indian tale type, but the issue of whether or not it is a fairy tale has not been discussed.

The term *fairy tale* is actually a poor one anyway, for fairies rarely appear in fairy tales. The vast majority of stories with fairies in them are classified by folklorists as belonging to the legend genre, not folktale. So since the term *fairy tale* is so inadequate, it is not clear that there is any advantage in forcing the folktales of other peoples and cultures into such a . . . misnomer. Regardless of whether or not one wants to extend the notion of fairy tale to African and American Indian folktales, the fact remains that *folktale* as a folklore genre is a universal one—even if specific tale types do not demonstrate universal distribution. This emphasizes the unduly restrictive nature of treatments of folktale which in effect ignore the rich folktale traditions of so much of the world.

Central Themes of Classical Fairy Tales

Max Lüthi

In *The Fairy Tale as Art Form and Portrait of Man,*
Max Lüthi says the conflict between appearance and
reality, one of the major philosophical dilemmas of
mankind, is the theme at the heart of the fairy tale. It
pervades the genre on many levels. Below the surface of the simple tales lies deep meaning and message, and a character with a beastly outer form may
have the soul of a prince. Closely linked to this major theme is the positive irony of the events of fairy
tales, where evil intention can inadvertently bestow
good fortune on innocent heroes. A professor emeritus of European Folk Literature at the University of
Zurich in Switzerland, Lüthi has written extensively
on the fairy tale style in *Once Upon a Time: On the
Nature of Fairy Tales.*

There are themes which crop up time and again in the fairy-
tale: readiness to help, die, or fight; the wish to do harm; the
human world is not in order; dangers threaten from within
the family, from within one's circle of friends, even from
within oneself; there is nothing impossible, no problem is
unsolvable; essential help comes from otherworldly (or unknown) powers; the small and the weak can triumph over
the large and the strong; justice prevails; appearances are
deceptive. Other themes are encountered less frequently:
poverty perverts (the parents of Hansel and Gretel—more often the theme is "wealth corrupts": the rich vs. the poor
brother or neighbor, the rich vs. the poor sister, etc.); justice
should be tempered with mercy; destiny is inevitable.

The selection of themes from the total number of possibilities and the frequency with which they appear contribute to the constitution of the fairytale as genre—and to

the determination of the world and the portrait of man which appear in it. They are at the same time of esthetic significance: Their numerous modifications offer variety, and the predominance, the ubiquity, of certain larger themes helps to give both individual narratives and the entire genre a certain measure of uniformity.

APPEARANCE VERSUS REALITY

Among all the themes mentioned, it is the conflict between *appearance and reality* which stands in first place in the fairytale. Setting aside the introductory formulas that play with appearance and reality, one can see the theme represented first purely in terms of surface features: The underestimated youngest, the neglected stepdaughter, the scald-head (who in reality has golden hair), the kitchen maid, and similar "dark figures" are among the favorite and most common fairytale heroes and heroines. The term *unpromising hero* is found in the Anglo-Saxon context. In addition to these "unpromising heroes" and heroines, who all have more to them than meets the eye, there are *unpromising helpers* (unprepossessing old men and women, little gray men, and animals) . . . and *unpromising things*. There are also *apparently* unaccomplishable tasks, not only those which are insoluble given realistic expectations and which with the help of magic are accomplished in the twinkling of an eye . . . , but also the commissions that are intended to bring about the death of the hero . . . and, contrary to expectation, bring him good fortune (the irony associated with the child of fortune); the dangerous demons and animals and revolting things which, in contradiction to all appearances, become helpers, etc. The situation is similar yet different with helper figures of the Faithful John sort: They appear suddenly to be unfaithful or treacherous, but precisely that which appears to be cruel faithlessness is the essence of true loyalty. Female sufferers on the Patient Griselda model, like the sister of the six swans, who carries out the difficult task which leads to the disenchantment of her brothers . . . bravely acquiesce in appearing to have killed and even devoured their own children, and despite all the injustice which they, their children, and finally also their husbands suffer as a result, they remain adamant and accept the false appearance right to the last—the explanation here comes from some other source, while the Faithful John figure finally reveals everything himself. . . . Appearances are also deceptive in the case of beautiful princesses who dance their shoes to pieces every night: They are, in contradiction to their beautiful exterior, bound up with monsters or demonic otherworldly beings—and such is the case with all the other beauties whose bodies are full of snakes, worms, or vermin. . . . But their being associated with evil is in a deeper sense also just appearance: Those who are bound to underworld demons can be released through the killing of the demon, those infested with worms can be cured by an operation; both can thus be returned to their true nature—the evil spell was just that, an evil spell. With Snow White's beautiful stepmother (or mother) and corresponding figures in other fairytales, the beauty is, in another sense, only appearance. The queen is not, as she thinks, the most beautiful in the land, she is only the second most beautiful; and thus, to her at least, her entire beauty has become worthless, pointless, only the appearance of beauty.

A PERVASIVE THEME

The latter are peripheral instances of the theme of appearance versus reality. But precisely because the theme is central to the fairytale, it has the most subtle ramifications. The portrayal of the conflict between appearance and reality is characteristic of the fairytale as genre. In no other genre of folk literature does it appear so frequently and in so many and various forms. This fact has not only esthetic but also anthropological significance: Since the central significance of the relationship between appearance and reality has been recognized or felt both in philosophy from the ancient Greeks up through [German philosopher Immanuel] Kant and into our own times and in individual literature from Sophocles' *Oedipus Rex* up through manneristic and baroque literature and again into our own times, it is certainly noteworthy that this theme in particular is all-pervasive in the simple fairytale. Man, by his very nature, is confronted with the problem of appearance versus reality. . . . "Gradually it filled me with dread to observe how similar are appearance and reality" wrote Conrad Ferdinand Meyer on noticing how perfectly the flight of a gull was mirrored in the sea. "And you, are you really provided with wings? Or only painted and reflected?" Meyer is a [German] poet who sees death and life as neighboring, as confusable with one another. The ancient statue dug up in the garden which the girl takes to be a god of love is in reality the god of death. The theme of appearance/reality is even more universally present in the fairytale than in Meyer—but in the fairytale everything is set at a distance. Nonpathetically, without causing "dread," it presents an aspect of the basic condition of man. *At a distance* also suggests the esthetic significance of the play of appearance versus reality. The unequivocalness which is peculiar to the fairytale—"black and white contrasts" extreme completeness of form, the partial equation of beautiful with good, on the one hand, and ugly with bad, on the other—is toned down by the multifarious playing off of appearance against reality, which, of course, is one of the basic principles of art and the esthetic in general. This playing off can enter in as early as the opening formula. Even the simple "Once upon a time" is ambiguous; behind the expression shimmers an opposite meaning: Oriental fairytales often begin with the formula "It was or not," while Hungarian ones enjoy beginning with "Where was it, where wasn't it" plus a surrealistic place designation ("In back of the beyond"—in the middle of a white flea), by means of which, in the words of [German folklorist] Gyula Ortutay, "the plot moves into the nonreal." A Rumanian fairytale may begin "Once upon a time as has never been, for if it hadn't happened, one wouldn't tell about it," or, even more direct, "When the poplar bore pears and the willow violets, when the bears fought each other using their tails". . . . [German writer] Mihai Pop emphasizes, certainly with justification, that the opening formulas are intended to lead one from the real into a nonreal world, the closing formulas from the nonreal back into the real. The tendency of the fairytale of magic to establish such a frame is in accord with its inclination to clarity of form, to the classical, in the stylistic sense. But these formulas are, in addition, the overture and finale to a piece in which the theme of appearance versus reality rings throughout.

Other Major Themes

Other important themes—important in and of themselves and frequent in the fairytale—are closely related to the theme of appearance versus reality. Such is the case with the theme of the *victory of the weak over the strong* and that of the *reversal.* The little man conquers the dragon or the giant, and the youngest (thus the weakest) and dumbest (he is generally only seemingly stupid, but he can also actually be stupid, especially in the farce fairytale) shows himself to be superior to his brothers, just as is the case with the mistreated youngest daughter or stepdaughter with respect to her better-treated siblings, and with unpromising things with respect to shiny ones. The apparently ordinary, small, weak, or ugly triumphs over the apparently—or even actually— big, strong, powerful, or beautiful. And here the possibility of reversal is already apparent: The advantaged change places with the disadvantaged. In animal tales, the smaller animal defeats the larger, thus the hedgehog defeats the rabbit, the crab the fox. In many fairytales the poor boy becomes prince consort or king. The disgust or anxiety of the bride or husband of an animal mate turns into love. The helper turns into an opponent, hence the devil who aids the poor man to gain wealth but then takes away his child, or Rumpelstiltskin, who helps the heroine in time of need but then also wishes to have her child, or even her, for himself. On the other hand, the opponent or apparent opponent can become a helper or a beloved mate: directly, as with the animal bridegroom . . . or indirectly, as with every antagonist who intends to harm the hero or heroine but ends up helping in the attempt. Situations can also be subject to reversal: The birthday celebration of Sleeping Beauty unexpectedly leads to harm instead of well-being; people turned to stone are revivified in a single stroke; the child of fortune who is supposedly sent to his death by the king or some rich man . . . ends up instead married to the daughter of the king or rich man—and this rich man, who again tries to arrange the death of the hero, is himself pushed into the lime pit as a result of his order's being carried out; he has laid the groundwork for his own demise. . . . There is irony here, as in many of the other reversals mentioned.

IRONY IN FAIRY TALES

Irony flashes in the opening and closing formulas of the fairytale and in several—partially traditional, partially improvised—incidental remarks of the narrator or individual fairytale figures. But far more important is the irony at work in *what happens* in the fairytale. One can speak of irony anyplace where what happens is the opposite of what those affected have strived for or expected. One speaks of tragic irony, where things are really worse than one believes. . . . Word irony, *rhetorical irony*, is mostly mocking, disillusioning, and negative; and sequential irony, *the irony of event*, is known to us mainly in the form of tragic irony, something thus also negative. Therefore, I prefer to call the rarer positive variety of irony *contrary irony*. It occurs infrequently in literature, just as it does in life—but it is the predominant variety in the fairytale, as one might expect, given the cheery character of the genre. Even in the fairytale, of course, it is clear that good, or what is intended to be good, can ironically lead to evil: The celebration after the birth of Sleeping Beauty, which is intended to bestow blessings on the child, leads to her enchantment; a father's intention of fulfilling the strange wish of his youngest daughter causes harm. But the fairytale often brings forth the opposite configuration. Evil leads to good (just as in both of the examples just mentioned everything turns out well after all). That has already become apparent in our presentation up to this point. The irony of fate predestines that the messenger carrying a letter intended to bring about his death should not only be spared but advance in the world: He marries the daughter of the one who has commissioned the intended crime, and it is just as if the latter had arranged for it to happen. On the way, the boy quite superfluously also falls into the hands of robbers. But even here the letter that is intended to do away with him saves him: The robbers open it, it arouses their orneriness, and instead of killing the messenger who has been sentenced to death, as they would have done under normal circumstances, they rewrite the letter intended to bring about harm as a letter leading to benefits . . . In the fairytale, however, the irony of fate, true contrary irony, rules: The letter commissioning the murder works counterproductively; the robbers succumb to a sort of contrary suggestion; while the tired hero is sleeping peacefully in spite of the warning of the old housekeeper ("when they come home, then they'll kill you . . ."), fate is working for him. Things turn out otherwise than as planned; the evil letter writer himself brings about exactly what he seeks to avoid—negative irony is directed against him. In the second part of the fairytale, he dashes headlong to his own destruction, sometimes as a result of unsuccessful imitation of his successful son-in-law, sometimes as a result of a new attempt to commission the murder, which then backfires on him (death in the lime pit). The situation of the boy sleeping unconcerned in the house of murderers is reminiscent of another with which we are already familiar: the fairytale hero who is assigned unaccomplishable tasks in the otherworld by an evil demon; for him, as well, they are accomplished while he is sleeping, ironically by the demon's own daughter. In the fairytale not only the same figures and situations turn up time and time again, but also the same models, though in many and various modifications. That a demon should kill his own children instead of the strangers he intends to kill . . . is also irony. The negative irony in the fairy tale is mainly directed against evil-doers: They meet their deaths in their own ovens, through their own tools, or through their own methods, or, as in Perrault's "Petit Poucet [The Little Thumbling]" they kill their own daughters or wives. Snow White, of course, thus a sympathetically drawn figure, also harms herself, bringing about her own death or apparent death— but it is just this "death" which then brings her the prince; and here contrary irony again comes into play: The clumsiness (stumbling) of the servants or, in other variants, their anger about the fact that they have to serve a dead maiden— one angrily strikes her—causes the bit of apple which Snow White has choked on to come back up, and the girl wakes from her death sleep. It is also a sort of irony when in certain variants of Cinderella the son of the house sets out to seek the beautiful girl, with no idea that he can—and finally will— find her at the place where he started, at home. Above all, however, one finds irony interwoven with the problem of appearance vs. reality: It is irony, even positive irony, that, contrary to all expectations and arrangements, the despised and the maltreated time and again end up emerging as winners, and that they finally outshine those in whose shadows they have stood. The dominance of such contrary irony in the fairytale is not accidental, and its effects are not random; it is an indispensable contributing factor to the view of the world and portrait of man which we encounter in the fairytale. . . .

MANIPULATION BY FAIRYTALE CHARACTERS

Just as the phenomenon of *self-injury* and *self-destruction* belongs to the area of irony, so also does the phenomenon of *manipulation*. We have run into manipulations, clever uses of scene management by individual figures, a number of times already. Gretel maneuvers the man-eating witch into her own oven; she is able to only because—and herein lies the irony—the witch shows Gretel, who pretends to be stupid, how one can creep into the oven or get shoved inside. Manipulation is not the same as ordering something done; as with irony, it is a matter of indirectness. The behind-the-scenes manipulation turns others into puppets, but in such a way that—and again it is precisely herein that the irony lies—they think they are acting independently and of their own free will. In the Ölenberg manuscript, the witch says to Gretel, "Sit on the board, I'll shove you into the oven. See if the bread is about done." The girl, however, says to her: "I don't understand. You sit on it first and I'll shove you in." The old woman sits on it, and the little sister pushes her in, closes the door and the witch gets burned up. . . .

The trick with the nightcap, a prototype already represented in ancient Greece, has become familiar especially through Perrault's "Petit Poucet": The tiny Thumbling puts the little golden crowns of the ogre's seven sleeping daughters on his own head and those of his brothers, and the caps of the boys on the sleeping daughters, in order to decoy the bloodthirsty father to his own (already bloodthirsty) children, so that he will cut their throats during the night instead of those of the seven boys, as is his real intention. In countless versions of "Bluebeard," the third sister manages to manipulate the murderer so that he carries the resurrected victims and finally her, as well, back home on his own back without knowing or wishing to do so. Thus the themes of appearance versus reality and of self-injury intertwine in many and various ways with the model of manipulation and the phenomenon of irony. In the fairytale, one constantly runs into manipulations, into examples of scene management in which other figures are unknowingly turned into puppets, very much in accord with the frequency of this particular phenomenon in actual human relations. To this degree, the fairytale is "realistic." Animal fairytales, fables, and religious fairytales also display such realistic nonrealism: Small and weak animals manipulate the large and strong, since it is precisely the weak that have reason to use indirect control. The strong can achieve a great deal without using detours; of course, not everything—often they also use scene management, whether for demagogical or for pedagogical reasons. There is a lot of high spirits and mischievousness in such scene management and manipulation—and for good reason:

Man is by nature a manager and manipulator through and through; he manipulates others, he manipulates nature, and he even manipulates himself. And since he is one who is initially weak, in comparison with the powers of nature and of many who surrounded him, especially his parents, it is obvious that he should also generally attribute the successful manipulations in the world of his narratives to the disadvantaged. He identifies with them not only if he is himself socially, economically, or politically underprivileged, but simply because of his role as man; he fully enjoys the manipulations in the narratives in a playful and good-humored way. Scene management and manipulations are also assigned to the secondary figures in the fairytale, to the negatively represented antagonists, who can enjoy great success for a while but who in the end still fail. . . . The strings which the scene managers pull, completely contrary to their expectations, lead the manipulated not to destruction but to even greater successes. Thus the irony-oriented basic pattern . . . becomes apparent: The evil-doers, with all their machinations, end up achieving the opposite of what they want; their intrigues result in benefits for their victims, not harm, and they themselves go under as a result of their own maneuvers (the self-destructiveness of evil). . . .

VARIATIONS ON A THEME

We have here encountered the predominant themes which interact to give the fairytale its particular character. The cardinal theme of the conflict between appearance and reality is reflected in the change of situations, conditions of existence, and forms of appearance into radically different ones, changes presented in the form of sudden transformations, enchantments and disenchantments, and also in the rising and falling of personal fortunes, in the shift from poverty to riches, or from servant status to kingdom, and in many another. If sequences can be seen as a transposing of juxtapositions onto the time axis, then the change of one situation into its opposite, of a condition into one completely different, is a factoring of the appearance/reality complex, a translation of the contradictory simultaneity into a contrastive sequence. As in the case of manipulation (the scene manager/puppet model), both the conflict between appearance and reality and the change into something opposite or in some way different are tied up with irony, which itself belongs to the features characterizing the fairytale and which comes out especially clearly in the also-emphasized theme of self-injury, self-destruction. That evil-doers, without knowing it, have to pronounce their own death sentences is characteristic: They are the cause of their own destruction. And that the weak are able to triumph over the strong, the small over the large, is again an expression of the all-pervasive theme of appearance versus reality.

The Meaning of Enchantment

Iona and Peter Opie

In *The Classic Fairy Tales,* British folklorists Iona and
Peter Opie compiled the first collection of the most
popular fairy tales, as they originally appeared in the
English language. In the following extract from the
introduction to the book, the Opies demonstrate how
many fairy tales as they are now known are 'prettified abridgements' of older, deeper, philosophical
tales. Unlike these newest variants which tend to
rely on transformation of the central characters
through acts of magic, the older forms focus on a
"disenchantment" or breaking of the spell which
kept the characters' true and noble natures hidden.

When the wonderful happens, when a holiday abroad is a
splendid success or an unlikely romance ends happily, we
commonly exclaim it was 'just like a fairy tale', overlooking
that most events in fairy tales are remarkable for their un-
pleasantness, and that in some of the tales there is no happy
ending, not even the hero or heroine escaping with their life.
Very possibly the story we have in mind is the story of Cinderella, as we imagine it to be, or have seen it in a prettified
abridgement: the story of a poor, hard-working drudge—
who we are certain represents ourselves—who is transformed by magic into a beauty, a social success, the belle of
the ball, the charmer who brings a king's heir-apparent literally to her feet.

REALITY MADE EVIDENT

We forget that in the story Perrault told, which is the basis of
virtually all subsequent retellings in English, Cinderella is
not any ordinary girl being scrubbed clean, dressed sump-
tuously, and endowed with virtues before being conveyed to

a gathering of her social superiors. Her story is not one of rags to riches, or of dreams come true, but of reality made evident. Despite Cinderella's menial position in the opening scene—a position she accepts with dignity and good humour—Cinderella is in fact her father's heir, she has been stated already to be 'of unparalleled goodness', she has as much right by position and birth to be at the ball as have others who have been invited, and no fairy godmother was required to make her beautiful. Her clothes only, not her features, are transformed by the magic wand; her feet do not become large after midnight; and the courtier who comes from the palace searching for the unidentified guest recognizes her beauty despite the shabbiness of her attire, and urges she should be allowed to try on the glass slipper.

In the most-loved fairy tales, it will be noticed, noble personages may be brought low by fairy enchantment or by human beastliness, but the lowly are seldom made noble. The established order is not stood on its head. Snow White and Sleeping Beauty are girls of royal birth. Cinderella was tested, and found worthy of her prince. The magic in the tales (if magic is what it is) lies in people and creatures being shown to be what they really are. The beggar woman at the well is really a fairy, the beast in 'Beauty and the Beast' is really a monarch, the frog is a handsome prince, the corpse of Snow White a living princess. Fairy tales are unlike popular romances in that they are seldom the enactments of dream-wishes. We would ourselves be unwilling to face the hazards the heroes have to face, even if we were certain, as the heroes are not, of final reward. Indeed, in fairy tales wishes are rarely granted; and when they are the wisher may be made to look as foolish as King Midas. He finds he has wished a sausage onto the end of his wife's nose, or that he himself has acquired an embarrassment of sexual organs. Stringent conditions may be laid down before a wish is granted: a mother must pledge her first born, a gay cavalier marry one who is repugnant to him. Even Cinderella's licence expires after a few hours. Enchantment, in practice, is the opposite to the golden dream. The wonderful happens, the lover is recognized, the spell of misfortune is broken, when the situation that already exists is utterly accepted, when additional tasks or disappointments are boldly faced, when poverty is seen to be of no consequence, when unfairness is borne without indignation, when the loathsome is loved. Perhaps, after all, fairy tales are to be numbered amongst the most philosophic tales that there are.

THE ROLE OF MAGIC IN SPECIFIC TALES

Further analysis may show the tales to be even less like the popular conception of them . . . . 'Little Red Ridinghood' and 'The Three Bears' have nothing magical about them other than that the animals behave to a greater or lesser degree like human beings, and are able to speak, an accomplishment which comes as no surprise to students of Aesop. The tale of Bluebeard contains a single magical incident (the reappearance of blood on the key to the forbidden chamber), an incident inessential to the story. Two further tales, 'The Three Wishes' and 'The Princess on the Pea', are definitely magical, but they are magical for a work-a-day purpose, they are fables rather than tales of romance. The long stories about Tom Thumb, Jack the Giant Killer, and Jack the Beanstalk Climber, the three best-known tales that are indigenous to Britain, although packed with fantastical happenings, are only incidentally romances. In essence they are simple adventure stories, as is the tale of that dressed-up cheat Puss in Boots. Two further adventure stories are 'Hansel and Gretel' and 'Hop o' my Thumb'. They concern peaceful characters of humble origin, who have no desire to battle with ogres, but who, when put to it, use native wit to outsmart the forces of evil. The stories of 'Rumpelstiltskin' and 'The Twelve Dancing Princesses' might almost be classed along with them, as describing two further skirmishes with the supernatural; but in the versions given by the Grimm brothers they are both stories in which the reader is singularly uninterested in the fate of the principal character. However, in the stories that are central to the fairy-tale tradition, the tales of royal romance and magical transformation—tales which are mostly of great age, and all of which are in one way or another related to each other— we find ourselves closely identifying with the principal characters. These characters are Cinderella, Snow White, Sleeping Beauty, the unnamed heroine of 'Diamonds and Toads', the King of Colchester's daughter in 'The Three Heads in the Well', Beauty in 'Beauty and the Beast', and the young princess in 'The Frog Prince'.

With Cinderella, whose story is at least one thousand years old, we have not only a girl who is worthy of becoming a princess, as has already been suggested, but a girl who is being supernaturally *prevented* from becoming a princess. When her situation is closely examined, particularly with the aid of parallels from different countries, she is seen to be under enchantment not when she is in her beauteous state, for that is her natural condition, but when she is in her *kitchen state*. Perrault's story, for all its wit and compassion, is a worldly and somewhat sentimentalized version of older, darker stories, which have many strange undertones. For instance, in a number of the variants it is apparent that the magical assistance the heroine receives comes to her from the spirit of her dead mother. Indeed, there are analogous tales in which the mother is also the indirect cause of the girl's distressed condition. In these stories the girl, who is often already a princess, has been obliged to leave her royal home and take kitchen employment elsewhere, due to a terrifying circumstance. Her mother, on her deathbed, has commanded her father not to marry again until he finds a woman who is as lovely as herself, or who possesses a finger so delicate it will fit her ring. After much searching the father, a king, realizes there is only one person as beautiful as was his wife, or with the ability to wear the ring, and this is his own daughter, whom he determines to marry. Hence the girl's flight.

In the story of Snow White, who also suffers because of her beauty, the fact of her being under a spell during her formative years (from the age of seven to, probably, fifteen) is more obvious than in Cinderella's case. During these years she is laid out in a coffin apparently dead. Release from the enchantment can be effected, it is evident, only through the seemingly unlikely event of someone (necessarily of royal birth?) falling in love with her lifeless body. The explanation that she comes to life through the piece of poisoned apple falling from her lips when her body is moved, poetic though the notion may be, is a mere rationalization; as can be seen by comparing her history with that of Sleeping Beauty, who we are explicitly told is under a spell, and whose sleeping body must necessarily be discovered by a king's son, or, in an earlier text, be raped by a king, if she is to be freed from the enchantment that has kept her in a coma for a hundred years.

In [Perrault's tale], 'Diamonds and Toads', and more especially in [an eighteenth century English equivalent], 'The

Three Heads in the Well' . . . we are at the heart of fairy-tale morality, where girls in a distressed state yet possess the charity to care for the condition of others. In 'The Three Heads in the Well' a princess willingly picks up one dismembered head after another, washing it, and combing its hair, and laying it down gently, actions requiring the courage, and the tranquil acceptance of a surprising situation, which it is well known many women do possess in an emergency. Thus, when the compassion of the King of Colchester's daughter [the tale's heroine] is appreciated, her relationship to Beauty in 'Beauty and the Beast' becomes clear, as also to the heroine of the more explicit tale of 'The Frog Prince', in which the girl has to let the frog have intercourse with her before the creature can be revealed to be a prince. These two tales are, then, the counterparts of Snow White and Sleeping Beauty, the roles of the sexes being reversed.

TRANSFORMATION THROUGH LOVE, NOT MAGIC

In these deeply-penetrating tales, fairy godmothers do not suddenly materialize, waving wands that make everything come right. The power of the godmothers is limited. Sometimes all they are able to offer is advice. They are never able, it seems, to change a worldly situation, or alter a wicked heart. What they can do, on occasion, is assist in the breaking of a spell or in the alleviation of its ill effect. In the story of Cinderella, the most interesting of the tales since the spell is the least apparent, we are repeatedly told, in variants, firstly of the girl's essential goodness; and, secondly, not only of the poor and even ridiculous clothes she wears, the rags, the grey bedgown, the garment made of rushes, but of her dirtiness—a condition we would not expect of the kind of person we know her to be, no matter how humble her employment, were she not, as she is, under a spell to appear sluttish. Nobody outside her family, it is apparent, must know she is other than a menial until a prince, who has only a sign to go by, finds her, as if guided by a star, and offers himself to her while she is still in her unattractive state. Further, she herself must behave as if she was a menial. The reason she returns home before midnight is to ensure that not even members of her family shall associate her with the vision of virtue and loveliness they have been admiring at the ball. The prince's admiration of her in her party dress is worthless. It is essential he plights himself to her while she is a kitchen maid, or the spell can never be broken. . . . On the face of it the message of the fairy tales is that transformation to a state of bliss is effected not by magic, but by the perfect love of one person for another. Yet clearly even this is not the whole story. The transformation is not an actual transformation but a disenchantment, the breaking of a spell. In each case we are aware that the person was always noble, that the magic has wrought no change in the person's soul, only in his or her outward form. In fairy tales there is no saving of the wicked in heart. Their fate is to have inflicted on them the evil they would inflict on others. The tub filled with toads and vipers shall become the murderous queen's final resting place.

Heroes and Heroines in Grimms' Fairy Tales

Maria Tatar

In the provocative work *The Hard Facts of Grimms' Fairy Tales,* Maria Tatar, professor of German Literature at Harvard University, explodes many of the commonly held beliefs about fairy tales. In the following extract, popular conceptions of the fairy tale hero as bold, brave and undaunted are dispelled. Through careful analysis of several tales, Tatar demonstrates that the acquired strengths of compassion and humility are the key to the hero's accession to wealth and power, suggesting that even the least talented youth might triumph over all.

Identifying fairy-tale heroes by name is no mean feat. In the Grimms' collection, only one in every ten actually has a name. But it is also no secret that the most celebrated characters in fairy tales are female. Cinderella, Snow White, Little Red Riding Hood, and Sleeping Beauty: these are the names that have left so vivid an imprint on childhood memories. With the exception of Hansel, who shares top billing with his sister, male protagonists are exceptionally unmemorable in name, if not in deed. Lacking the colorful descriptive sobriquets (nickname or assumed name) that accord their female counterparts a distinctive identity, these figures are presented as types and defined by their parentage (the miller's son), by their station in life (the prince), by their relationship to siblings (the youngest brother), by their level of intelligence (the simpleton), or by physical deformities (Thumbling).

Most people may be at a loss when it comes to naming fairy-tale heroes, but few have trouble characterizing them. "In song and story," writes Simone de Beauvoir (French feminist writer), "the young man is seen departing adventurously in search of woman; he slays the dragon, he battles giants." And what are this young man's attributes? One commentator on the Grimms' collection describes him as "active, competitive, handsome, industrious, cunning, acquisitive." That list sums up the conventional wisdom on the dragon slayers and giant killers of fairy-tale lore.

HEROES NOT HEROIC

The conventional wisdom, however, proves to be fairy tale so far as German folklore is concerned. A reading of the first edition of the *Nursery and Household Tales* reveals that there are exactly two dragon slayers and only one giant killer in the entire collection of some 150 tales. One of those stories, "Johannes-Wassersprung and Caspar-Wassersprung," rehearses the classic story of the slaying of a seven-headed dragon and the liberation of a princess, but (for unknown reason) the tale never made it to the second edition of the *Nursery and Household Tales.* The other dragon-slaying hero bears the distinctly unheroic name Stupid Hans (Dummhans), and the contest in which he dispatches three dragons, each with a different number of heads, is less than gripping. As for the giant killer, he succeeds in decapitating three giants, but only because the proper sword is placed directly in his path. If there is any attribute that these heroes share, it is naiveté. Like so many other heroes in the Grimms' collection, they are decidedly unworldly figures. "Innocent," "silly," "useless," "foolish," "simple," and "guileless": these are the adjectives applied repeatedly to fairy-tale heroes in the Grimms' collection.

Among folklorists, it is the fashion to divide heroes into two distinct classes. There are active heroes and passive heroes, "formal heroes" and "ideal heroes," dragon slayers and male Cinderellas, tricksters, and simpletons. According to theory, the oppositions active/passive, seeker/victim, brave/timid, and naive/cunning serve as useful guides for classifying fairy-tale heroes. In practice, though, it is not always easy to determine whether a hero relies on his own resources or depends on helpers. Does he have a zest for danger or does he simply weather the various adventures that befall him? Just what is his level of intelligence? What at first blush appear to be straightforward choices turn out to be fraught with complexities. The happy-go-lucky simpleton who appears to succeed without trying is not always as doltish as his name or reputation would lead us to believe, and the roguish trickster does not always live up to his reputation for shrewd reasoning.

There is a further complication. Despite their seeming artlessness, the *Nursery and Household Tales* are not without occasional ironic touches that subvert surface meanings. In particular, the epithets and predicates (adjectives expressing a quality or trait) reserved for their protagonists can highlight utterly uncharacteristic traits. The heroine of "Clever Else" ranks high on the list of dull-witted characters; "Hans in Luck" charts a steady decline in its hero's fortunes; and the brave little tailor in the story of that title displays more bravado than bravery. In the world of fairy tales, a simpleton can easily slip into the role of a cunning trickster; a humble miller's son can become a king; and a cowardly fool can emerge as a stout-hearted hero. Character traits display an astonishing lack of stability, shifting almost imperceptibly into their opposites as the tale unfolds. Bearing this in mind, let us take the measure of male protagonists in the Grimms' collection to determine what character traits they share and to assess the extent to which the plots of their adventures follow a predictable course.

HEROES ARE NAIVE, WILLFUL, COWARDLY

If the female protagonists of fairy tales are often as good as they are beautiful, their male counterparts generally appear to be as young and naive as they are stupid. Snow White's stepmother may be enraged by her stepdaughter's superior beauty, but the fathers of male heroes are eternally exasperated by the unrivaled obtuseness of their sons. To the question, Who is the stupidest of them all? most fairy-tale fathers would reply: my youngest son. Yet that son is also the chosen son, the son who ultimately outdoes his older and wiser siblings. In an almost perverse fashion, fairy tales featuring male protagonists chart the success story of adolescents who lack even the good sense to heed the instructions of the many helpers and donors who rush to their aid in an attempt to avert catastrophes and to ensure a happy ending. "You don't really deserve my help," declares one such intercessor in frustration after his sage advice has been disregarded on no less than three occasions.

In fairy tales all over the world, the one least likely to succeed paradoxically becomes the one mostly likely to succeed. Merit rarely counts; luck seems to be everything. Aladdin, the prototype of the undeserving hero who succeeds in living happily ever after, begins his rise to wealth and power under less than auspicious circumstances. The introductory paragraphs of his tale give the lie to the view that classical fairy tales reward virtue and punish evil. "Once upon a time," begins the story "Aladdin and the Enchanted Lamp," "there lived in a certain city of China an impoverished tailor who had a son called Aladdin. From his earliest years this Aladdin was a headstrong and incorrigible good-for-nothing." When he grows older, he refuses to learn a trade and persists in his idle ways until his father, "grieving over the perverseness of his son," falls ill and dies. Yet this same Aladdin, who becomes ever more wayward after having dispatched his father to the grave, ultimately inherits a sultan's throne. As one critic correctly points out, the story of Aladdin and his enchanted lamp exalts and glorifies "one of the most undeserving characters imaginable." It is telling that Aladdin made his way so easily from the pages of German translations of *The Thousand and One Nights* to the oral narratives of one region of Germany. Once his exotic name was change to Dummhans, he was evidently quickly assimilated into Pomeranian folklore, so much so that it was difficult to distinguish him from native sons.

The heroes of the *Nursery and Household Tales* may, for the most part, be unlikely to win prizes for intelligence and good behavior, but they are even less likely to garner awards for courage. Their stories chronicle perilous adventures, but they often remain both cowardly and passive. When summoned to discharge the first in a series of three tasks, the simpleton in "The Queen Bee" simply sits down and has a good cry. In "The Three Feathers," the hero sits down and "feels sad" instead of rising to the challenges posed by his father. Fairy tale heroines have never stood as models of an enterprising spirit, but it is also not rare for fairy-tale heroes to suffer silently and to endure hardships in a hopeless passive fashion.

COMPASSION AND HUMILITY REWARDED

For all their shortcomings, the simpletons in the Grimms' fairy tales possess one character trait that sets them apart from their fraternal rivals: compassion. That compassion is typically reserved for the natural allies and benefactors of fairy-tale heroes: the animals that inhabit the earth, the waters, and the sky. Even before the simpleton embarks on a journey to foreign kingdoms or undertakes diverse tasks to liberate a princess, he must prove himself worthy of assistance from nature or from supernatural powers by displaying compassion. Of the various tests, tasks, and trials imposed on a hero, this first test figures as the most important, for it establishes his privileged status. Once he exhibits compassion—with its logical concomitant of humility—he can do no wrong, even when he violates interdictions, disregards warnings, and ignores instructions. This preliminary test of the hero's character comes to serve the dual function of singling out the hero from his brothers and of furnishing him with potential helpers for the tasks that lie ahead.

Two fairy tales from the Grimms' collection illustrate the extent to which compassion is rewarded. In "The Queen Bee," the youngest of three sons defends an anthill, a bevy of ducks, and a beehive from the assaults of his mischievous brothers. "Leave the animals alone," he admonishes his elders on three occasions. Compassion pays off in the end, for this youngest son is also the one to escape being turned to stone—a punishment that perfectly suits the crimes of his callous siblings. With the help of his newly won allies, the simpleton of the family discharges three "impossible" tasks written for him on a stone slab. He gathers a thousand pearls that lie strewn about the forest, fetches a bedroom key from the sea's depths, and succeeds in identifying the youngest of the three "completely identical" sisters. To be more precise, the ants gather the pearls, the ducks fetch the keys, and the bees identify the youngest sister. Yet the simpleton is credited with disenchanting the palace in which the trio of princesses resides; he thereby wins the hand of the youngest and earns the right to give the other two sisters in marriage to his brothers.

The hero of "The White Snake," like the simpleton of "The Queen Bee," hardly lifts a finger to win his bride. Once he displays compassion for wildlife by coming to the rescue of three fish, a colony of ants, and three ravens, he joins the ranks of the "chosen," who receive assistance from helpers as soon as they are charged with carrying out tasks. Although male fairy-tale figures have customarily been celebrated for their heroic feats, their greatest achievement actually rests on the passing of a character test. By enshrining compassion and humility, which—unlike intelligence and brute strength—are acquired characteristics rather than innate traits, the Grimms' tales make it clear to their implied audience (which gradually came to be adolescents) that even the least talented youth can rise to the top.

Once the hero has proven himself in the preliminary character test, he is braced for the tasks that lie ahead. The grateful beneficiaries of his deeds are quick to even out the balance sheet. As soon as the hero finds himself faced with an impossible task—emptying a lake with a perforated spoon, building and furnishing a castle overnight, devouring a mountain of bread in twenty-four hours—help is at hand. For every task that requires wisdom, courage, endurance, strength, or simply an appetite and a thirst of gargantuan proportions, there is a helper—or a group of helpers—possessing the requisite attributes. And ultimately the achievements of the helper redound to the hero, for he is credited with having drained the lake, built the castle, and consumed the bread.

PUNISHMENT OF TREACHERY

Passing the preliminary test and carrying out the basic tasks are sufficient to secure a princess and her kingdom. Nonetheless, a number of fairy tales mount a third act in keeping with the ternary principle governing their plots. The final trial the hero must endure is motivated by the reappearance of the fraternal rivals who vexed the hero in his earlier, preheroic days. The brothers seize the earliest opportunity to pilfer the hero's riches, alienate him from his beloved, malign his good name, or banish him from the land. Yet they are no match for the hero, who deftly outwits them and survives their assaults. Although the hero is rarely instrumental in carrying out the tasks imposed on him, in the end he acquires the attributes of his helpers and gains the strength, courage, and wit needed to prevail.

Just as the humble male protagonist matures and is elevated to a higher station in life, so his antagonists are demeaned and demoted in the final, optional segment of the tale. If the hero often distinguishes himself by showing mercy for animals, he remains singularly uncharitable when it comes to dealing with human rivals. "Off with everyone's head but my own," proclaims the hero of "The King of the Golden Mountain." And he makes good on the threat. Even brothers and brides are dispatched by fairy-tale heroes without a moment's hesitation once their deceit comes to light. The hero of "The Knapsack, the Hat, and the Horn," for example, does away with his wife once he uncovers her duplicity. Treachery is punished as swiftly and as predictably as compassion is rewarded. This third phase of the hero's career endows his story with a symmetry and balance for which all tales strive. Like the first two acts, the final act stages a contest between a youth and his two older, but morally inferior brothers. Both dramatic conflicts culminate in the rewarding of good will and the punishment of treachery; the last act simply intensifies the reward (a princess and a kingdom) and the punishment (death). In doing so, it adds not only moral resonance, but also a measure of finality to the tale. The hero has not only attained the highest office in the land, but has also eliminated his every competitor. For that office, he was singled out in the tale's first episode, made singular in the tale's second part, and celebrated as the sole and single heir to the throne in the tale's coda.

HEROES, HEROINES, AND HUMILITY

The trajectory of the hero's path leads him to the goal shared by all fairy tales, whether they chart the fortunes of male or female protagonists. In keeping with the fundamental law requiring the reversal of all conditions prevailing in its introductory paragraphs, the fairy tale ends by enthroning the humble and enriching the impoverished. The male heroes of fairy tales are humble in at least one, and often in both, senses of the term. More often than not they are low on the totem pole in families of common origins. But whether born to the crown or raised on a farm, they are also frequently humble in character; without this special quality they would fail to qualify for the munificence of helpers and donors. Thus, humility seems to be the badge of the fairy-tale hero. And since humbleness, in one of its shades of meaning, can inhere in members of any social class, both princes and peasants are eligible for the role of hero in fairy tales.

Humility also comes to color the psychological makeup of fairy-tale heroines. Female protagonists are by nature just as humble as their male counterparts, but they display that virtue in a strikingly different fashion and at a different point in their fairy-tale careers. Fairy tales often highlight psychological characteristics by translating them into elements of plot; in the case of female heroines, this proves especially true. Daughters of millers and daughters of kings alike are not merely designated as humble; they are actually humbled in the course of their stories. In fact, *humbled* is perhaps too mild a term to use for the many humiliations to which female protagonists must submit.

Since most fairy tales end with marriage, it seems logical to assume that a single tale suffices to illustrate the contrasting fates of male and female protagonists. Yet though there is often a happy couple at the end of a fairy tale, the fate of only a single, central character is at stake as the tale unfolds. That pivotal figure stands so firmly rooted at the center of events that all other characters are defined solely by their relationship to him and consequently lack an autonomous sphere of action. In "Cinderella," for instance, even the bridegroom, for all the dashing chivalry attributed to him by Walt Disney and others, remains a colorless figure. The tale tells us nothing more about him than that he is the son of a king. Lacking a history, a story, and even a name, he is reduced to the function of prince-rescuer waiting in the wings for his cue. The brides in stories of male heroes fare little better. Relegated to subordinate roles, they too fail to engage our interest. Still, there are exceptions to every rule, and the Grimms' collection provides one noteworthy variation on the principle that only one character can occupy center stage in fairy tales. "The Goose Girl at the Spring" weaves together the fates of both partners in the marriage with which it concludes. To be sure, there are signs that the tale is not of one piece, that at some historical juncture it occurred to one teller of tales to splice two separate plots. Nonetheless, the two plots conveniently dovetail to create a single narrative. The story of the humble count and the humbled princess who marries him offers an exemplary study in contrast between the lot of males and that of females in fairy tales culminating in wedding ceremonies.

FAIRY TALES CONTRAST HUMILITY IN HERO AND HEROINE

"The Goose Girl at the Spring" commences with an account of the heroine's future bridegroom. The young man is handsome, rich, and noble, yet he must—like the most lowly fairy-tale heroes—prove his mettle by displaying compassion and humility. Without these virtues, his otherwise impeccable credentials would prove utterly worthless. And indeed, we learn that the young count is not only able to "feel compassion," but that he is also, despite his noble station, not too proud to translate compassion into action. Once he demonstrates his humility by easing the burdens of a feeble old hag shunned by everyone else, he earns himself a passport to luck and success. Like his many artless benevolent folkloric kinsmen, the count becomes the recipient of a gift that accords him a privileged status among potential suitors of a princess. The emerald etui bestowed upon him by the old hag ultimately leads him to his bride—a princess masquerading as a shepherdess.

Neither the count nor his rustic bride can boast humble origins. The unsightly girl tending geese at the beginning of the tale is not at all what she seems. At the well, she peels off her rural costume along with her rough skin to reveal that she must be a princess. Despite her aristocratic origins, she too can ascend to a higher position, for her fairy-tale days are spent in the most modest of circumstances. Unlike her groom, however, she was pressed into assuming a humble position when her own father banished her from the household. Like countless folkloric heroines, she suffers a humiliating fall that reduces her from a princess to a peasant, from a privileged daughter to an impoverished menial. Fairy-tale heroes receive gifts and assistance once they actively prove their compassion and humility; heroines, by contrast, become the beneficiaries of helpers and rescuers only after they have been abased and forced to learn humility.

HUMILIATION OF THE FAIRY TALE HEROINE

There are many well-known tales of victimized female heroines who rise to or return to the ranks of royalty once they have been humbled and humiliated. But no tales more explicitly display the humiliation prerequisite to a happy ending than "King Thrushbeard," "The Mongoose," and "The Six Servants." King Thrushbeard's bride furnishes a classic example of the heroine who earns a king and a crown after straitened circumstances break her arrogance and pride. It is not enough that she curses the false pride that led her to her downfall; her husband must also solemnly state: "All of this was done to crush your pride and to punish you for the haughty way in which you treated me." When King Thrushbeard generously offers to reinstate her to a royal position,

she feels so deeply mortified that she declares herself un-
worthy to become his bride. The princess in the tale known
as "The Mongoose" also finds herself humbled by her prospective husband. Nonetheless, she takes the defeat in stride
and observes to herself with more than a touch of satisfac-
tion: "He is cleverer than you!" The princess-heroine of "The
Six Servants" is also cheerfully repentant and resigned to
her fate by the end of the story. Reduced to tending swine
with her husband (a prince who has duped her into believing that he is a peasant), she is prepared to accept her lot:
"I've only got what I deserved for being so haughty and
proud." After revealing the true facts of his life, her husband
justifies the deception by declaring: "I suffered so much for
you, it was only right that you should suffer for me."

As the tale "The Six Servants" makes clear, young men
"suffer" by taking the credit for tasks carried out by animal
helpers, human servants, or supernatural assistants. Women
suffer by being forced into a lowly social position. In short,
male heroes demonstrate from the start a meekness and humility that qualify them for an ascent to wealth, the exercise
of power, and happiness crowned by wedded bliss; their female counterparts undergo a process of humiliation and defeat that ends with a rapid rise in social status through marriage but that also signals a loss of pride and the abdication
of power.

CHAPTER 2

Writers and Collections of Fairy Tales

Fairy
Tales

Charles Perrault's
Mother Goose Tales

Michael Patrick Hearn

Some of the most familiar fairy tales of Western culture—"Cinderella," "Sleeping Beauty," "Puss-in-Boots" and "Little Red Riding Hood"—were first put into literary form in the late 17th century by French academician Charles Perrault. In his preface to Perrault's *Histories or Tales of Times Past* (also known as *Mother Goose Tales*), Michael Patrick Hearn says Perrault did not set out to merely record the tales he heard. Instead, while retaining the simplicity of style and structure found in the oral tradition, Perrault selected, embroidered, and refined specific fairy tales. His purpose was to deliver moral messages to his audience, specifically the children of the French court. The ethical power of the tales, and the grace and charm of Perrault's presentation is responsible for their enduring popularity. Michael Hearn is a writer and critic of children's literature.

The publication of *Histoires ou Contes du temps passé, avec des Moralitez* by Charles Perrault in January 1697 marked the beginning of a true literature written for children. Perrault did not merely collect the old stories (as did the Brothers Grimm); he adapted the folk material to his own theories of juvenile letters. Before his *contes de ma mère l'oye,*[1] most books written specifically for the young were treatises of theology, history, and manners, all now forgotten. The only other literature available to children was inherited from their parents' reading. This adult poetry and prose was often given to the young unexpurgated. Only Jean de La Fontaine's *Fables Choisies, mises en vers* (1668) precedes Perrault's work and is still a living piece of French juvenile literature,

1. a common expression in seventeenth century France meaning 'old wives' tales

Excerpted from the "Preface," by Michael Patrick Hearn, in *Histories or Tales of Times Past* (Garland: New York, 1977) by Charles Perrault. Copyright © 1977 by Michael Patrick Hearn. Reprinted with permission from the author.

but his Aesop in verse has now generally been replaced by other translations of the Greek fables. Although a few of the stories are popularly known in subsequent retellings, Perrault's collection of classic fairy tales is the earliest example of children's fiction still read (at least in France) as originally written.

PERRAULT'S ACHIEVEMENTS

Except for the Mother Goose tales, Perrault contributed nothing of consequence to French letters. He spent much of his professional life as a civil servant, as assistant superintendent of public works under Colbert. A dilettante, Perrault toyed with theology, medicine, architecture, law, poetry. His achievements were primarily social. He helped his brother Claude, a physician, found the Academy of Science. Although the great Roman architect Bernini had initially been contacted to complete the design of the Louvre, it was Charles Perrault who conceived the idea of the great east front of the palace (carried out by Claude), which is known as Perrault's Colonnade. He was also responsible for keeping the gardens of the Tuileries open to the French people and their children. Without much basis for the honor (he had written a few undistinguished verses), Perrault was elected to the French Academy.

Here he clumsily set off the famous academic battle of the Ancients and the Moderns. From childhood, Perrault preferred novelty to tradition; he was dismissed from the College de Beauvais for rebelling against his instructor's insistence on the authority of the classics. In his unremarkable poem "Le Siècle de Louis XIV," Perrault supported his praise of his fellow French artists by disparaging Homer and other masters of the past. His critical remarks caused a spirited debate in the Academy as to which was superior, the classical or the contemporary, an argument that has never been settled. . . .

IMITATING THE SIMPLICITY OF ORAL TRADITION

It was during his pensioned retirement that Perrault wrote his celebrated tales of Mother Goose. The French academician had fallen under the spell of the literary salon of Mlle. L'Héritier. Her circle of both ladies and gentlemen of the court entertained themselves with retelling old fairy stories, still preserved in the nurseries. Several members of the salon found those recounted by governesses told "in a most imperfect form," and Mme. D'Aulnoy may wait a hundred years or be merely a scullery maid, true love will find a way to the proper lover. The sexual symbolism is perhaps strongest in "Little Red Riding Hood." Perrault in this simple tale seems to have expanded a folk warning against talking to strangers into one against the honey-tongued young men who inhabited Versailles. The eating of Red Riding Hood suggests the obvious threat of rape to a virgin who carelessly shares her bed with the wrong person. Lest his meaning be missed, Perrault added morals in verse at the end of each story. Although Basile had done the same in his *cunti,* Perrault was more likely following the design of La Fontaine's retellings of Aesop.

FABLES INFLUENCE PERRAULT'S WORK

During the seventeenth century, the fable was considered an art form. Perrault followed the fashion by captioning a set of prints of the sculpted fountains in the gardens of Versailles with appropriate rephrasings of Aesop in prose and morals in verse as *Le Labyrinthe de Versailles* (1675). He also translated the Italian fables of Gabriello Faerno in 1699 and wrote at least one original fable in verse, "Les Souhaits Ridicules" (1693).

It was, however, La Fontaine's fables that he most admired. Perrault found these verses to be "Works of an incomparable Beauty, wherein there concurs an ingenious Simplicity, a sprightly Honesty, and an original Pleasantry, which never having any thing of cold, causes a surprise ever new." He recognized in these retellings that La Fontaine "join'd to the good sense of Esop, the Ornaments of his own invention, so suitable, so judicious, and so diverting at the same time, that it is difficult to read any thing more useful and more agreeable all together." The qualities Perrault admired in La Fontaine's work he emulated in his own retellings of past literature; like La Fontaine, Perrault "did not invent [them], but he chose them well, and made them almost always better than they were."

PERRAULT'S MORAL PURPOSE

Apparently what was most appealing to Perrault in these fables was that they were not only entertaining but also "useful." As Perrault explained in the preface to his 1695 collection of verse tales, "Is it not praiseworthy of fathers and mothers, when the children are not yet old enough to taste strong unpleasant truths, to make them . . . swallow them by enveloping them in tales that are pleasant and suited to their tender years? It is unbelievable how eagerly these innocent souls, whose natural goodness has not yet been corrupted, receive these subtle teachings." Aware of the proper education of the young, Perrault shared with [English philosopher] John Locke the revolutionary concept that learning need not be unpleasant to be effective. In the dedication to his published *contes,* Perrault stressed the ethical importance of his stories, each with "a very sensible moral." Although the delightful tale of "Cinderella" contains nothing particularly didactic, Perrault was able to disclose in his moral that grace of character has as great a magic power as a fairy's wand; even the deceit in "Puss in Boots" is tempered by finding in the story the proof that

> . . . youth, a good face, a good air and mien
> Are not always indifferent mediums to win
> The heart of the fair, and gently inspire
> The flames of tender passion, and tender desire.

In adding his morals, Perrault adapted traditional folklore to his own thoughts on education.

It was the ethical power in the stories that particularly interested his contemporaries in this age of fable. Robert Samber, in the dedication to his translation, the first in English, stressed Perrault's addition of these maxims, "knowing they tended to the Encouragement of Virtue, and the Depressing of Vice: the former of which is ever rewarded in them, and the latter ever punished, the true End and Design of Fable."

MORAL TEACHINGS AND NARRATIVE STYLE

Perrault, however, never allowed his teachings to come in conflict with the pacing of his narratives. His morals occasionally (as in "Puss in Boots") seem forced, and not surprisingly the stories are frequently reprinted without the secondary verses. Often Perrault includes two when one will suffice. In "Blue Beard" the second verse has less to do with the actual story and more to do with attitudes of the French court:

> . . . this is a story of long past,
> No husbands now such panick terrors cast;
> Nor weakly, with a vain despotick hand,

Imperious, what's impossible, command:
And be they discontented, or the fire
Of wicked jealousy their hearts inspire,
They softly sing; and of whatever hue
Their beard may chance to be, or black or blue,
Grizzled or russet, it is hard to say
Which of the two, the man or the wife, bears sway.

Such arbitrary observations, however, never weaken the grace and charm of his storytelling.

PERRAULT'S GRACEFUL STYLE

Perrault's prose displays none of the mannerisms inherent in most of the didactic books written for children before and immediately after the publication of his *contes*. His style (even when imbedded with provincialisms) remains fresh and spontaneous. Rarely does one find a distracting detail or an unnecessary description. The author's refined craft in perfecting his prose can be seen by a comparison between the original dedication manuscript of 1695 (now in the Pierpont Morgan Library) and the published collection. As the poet Marianne Moore observed, Perrault in preparing the tales for the press "saw ways of making them better." Some changes, just in a word or two, alter the author's perception of his characters. For example, in "Puss in Boots," *le chat* (the cat) of the manuscript becomes in the book *ce drôsle* (the rascal) when he steals his master's clothes and tells the king that the theft was the work of robbers. In the original "Little Red Riding Hood," Perrault merely concludes that the wolf ate her up; in the final version, he greatly enriches the scene by having the villain jump upon her and then eat her up. Some elaborations are more complex. In the earlier "Cinderella," he says only that she had to eat in the kitchen; but in the published form the true sadness of her condition is revealed: The stepmother "employed her in the meanest work of the house, she cleaned the dishes and stands, and rubbed Madam's chamber, and those of the young Madams her daughters: she lay on the top of the house in a garret, upon a wretched straw bed." These alterations fortunately never corrupt the character of the original style. In both manuscript and published book, the prose is as direct and smooth as the language of one of the old nurses at bedtime. Not surprisingly, it is Perrault's versions of the old stories that in numerous translations have entered the folk literature of many nations.

Charles Perrault was a true artist. By fulfilling his original literary purposes through a distinctive style, he created the first masterpiece of juvenile literature. His tales of Mother Goose will be read and reread as he wrote them wherever there is a hunger for things marvelous and true to the human soul.

Grimms' *Household Tales*

Linda Dégh

The Grimm brothers' *Household Tales*, first published in Germany in 1812, is the most often cited
source for many famous fairy tales ("Cinderella,"
"Sleeping Beauty," "Hansel and Gretel" among others). In the following extract, Linda Dégh says the
scholars were motivated by a romantic belief in the
superiority of the 'natural poetry' of the people, and a
deep desire to outline a national ideology to boost
cultural pride in a period of political turbulence in
Germany. The final product, however, was not an accurate recording of oral tales of the peasants, as the
Grimms maintained, nor were many of the tales of
German origin. Linda Dégh is professor of Folklore
at the Folklore Institute, Indiana University, and has
published many of the folktales of the peasants,
shepherds, fishermen and peddlers of the Hungarian
countryside, where she spent time as a child.

The unacquainted reader, looking at the German title of
Grimms' *Household Tales—Kinder-und Hausmärchen*—will
probably take for granted that it contains what it promises:
tales for the nursery and the household. Relying on traditional
knowledge passed on for over a century from generation to
generation of parents, grandparents, godparents, aunts, un-
cles, and grade school teachers, the reader will not be surprised to see several complete and abridged editions of this
book, year after year, as best sellers on the children's Christmas gift market. At closer scrutiny, however, he might be disappointed by the realization that the collection as a whole is
not for children and not for the household. Neither is it a ho-
mogeneous body of tales.

Excerpted from "Grimms' Household Tales and Its Place in the Household: The Social
Relevance of a Controversial Classic," by Linda Dégh, *Western Folklore*, vol. 38, no. 2,
April 1979. Copyright © 1979 by the California Folklore Society. Reprinted with per-
mission from the California Folklore Society.

CONTROVERSY OVER GRIMMS' TALES

What is it then? A bunch of various stories "written" by Jacob and Wilhelm Grimm? A historic marker to this effect was posted on a house in Kassel where the brothers lived during the creation of their collection. But the statement of the marker is not altogether true because the stories were more adapted than written, and some were adapted (or written) by the brothers, some by others. How is this possible? Were the stories not supposed to be folktales taken from the lips of oral tellers? Most of them were, but some were not. Were the transmitters of these stories peasants from the rural countryside? Not really, but if so, only indirectly. Are the Grimm tales, then, not original folk narratives? Some are, but most are not.

Is it true that, as the Grimms have contended, the tales are the late remains of an ancient Germanic mythology and heroic epic and thus belong to the treasure house of the national poetry of the German people? No, many of them were known earlier in many countries, as is evidenced by such famous collections as the *Arabian Nights,* Basile's *Pentamerone,* and Perrault's *Histoires ou Contes du temps passé, avec des moralitéz.* But then, are they at least prototypes of genuine oral narratives, since they seem to resemble tales known around the world from later sources? This is not quite so, or perhaps it is. More probably, the *Household Tales,* as a stylistically and ideologically standardized storybook, reinforced earlier narratives and influenced the formulation and the maintenance of tales in both oral and literary circulation . . . since the release of the first volume.

Attitudes toward the collection have been as ambiguous as the answers to the questions concerning the Grimms' work, and they have changed through time. Be that as it may, the appeal of the stories has never faded. While millions have enjoyed their enchanting spell, the Grimms' masterpiece has remained controversial. The spirit of controversy still lingers on.

NATIONALIST SENTIMENT

Jacob was twenty-one and Wilhelm twenty when in 1806 they began to collect tales. Like fellow romanticists of the post-Herder era, they recognized the superiority of *Naturpoesie* [nature poetry] "made by itself" through divine inspiration and uttered by the ignorant folk, over the *Kunstpoesie* [art poetry] constructed by poets. Their interest turned specifically toward the national poetry of the folk. Tales, songs, and beliefs of German peasants were, for the Grimms, splintered remnants of the mythology of pagan ancestors suppressed by the medieval church. Their aim was to reconstruct this mythology by piecing together the splinters for the education of the people. According to the brothers, language, religion, and poetry, as well as heroic virtues manifested in the ancestral epic, would make the Germans conscious of their national values and effective in the struggle for national survival and independence in their age of political turbulence. The gathering of tale materials, according to Jacob, would lead to a history of German poetry.

Encouraged by their fellow folk enthusiasts, Achim von Arnim and Clemens Brentano, collectors and publishers of folksongs, the two Grimms set to work. In the words of Jacob, they were determined to record authentic oral folktales "faithfully, true to the letter, including the socalled nonsensical speech dialect, mannerisms, turns of events, even if they seem grammatically incorrect." Folk narratives, seen by the Grimms as centuries-old national poems, included "stories from the entire German Fatherland: all traditions of common man, be they sad or merry, didactic or funny, especially the Märchen [fairy tales] of nurses and children, evening recounts and spinnery stories."

TALES NOT FROM GERMAN FOLK

With this original aim in mind, the brothers started to collect in their Hessen homeland, actively seeking the genuine arch-German peasant tradition as represented by the Hessen folk. In search of storytellers, they enlisted the help of relatives and childhood friends: first sister Lotte; then the daughters of their next-door neighbor, pharmacist Wild (one of whom, Dortchen, later became the wife of Wilhelm); and finally the children of the Hassenpflug family. Others were added to this small collecting team later, when the brothers made new acquaintances outside of their home. Among their many intellectual friends, the best contributors were the young members of the Haxthausen family and the Droste-Hülshoff sisters. These well-educated collectors from the affluent urban elite in many cases acted as retellers of stories remembered from childhood rather than as exacting recorders of what the Grimms were looking for among household servants, nursemaids, and simple peasants.

Until recently, it was generally accepted that the earliest among the authentic folk raconteurs was Old Marie, nanny of the Wild children, and that "Little Brother and Little Sister," "Red Riding Hood," "Godfather Death," "Briar Rose," "Robber Bridegroom," and "Snow White" were her contributions to the first edition of *Household Tales* in 1812. Close scrutiny of informants and their repertoires, however, has revealed recently that the housekeeper of the Wild family was probably no storyteller and that in mentioning Marie, the Grimms meant rather their friend, the young Marie Hassenpflug. Katharina Dorothea Viehmann was presented as

WHITEWASHING SNOW WHITE

In One Fairy Story Too Many: The Brothers Grimm and Their Tales, *John M. Ellis says that in their zeal to cater to middle class sensibilities, the Grimm brothers substantially altered oral fairy tales, robbing them of their powerful central themes. In the following extract he describes their revisions to the original "Snow White" tale.*

The fate of *Sneewwitchen (Snow-white)* as it progressed through the seven editions of Grimms' *Household Tales* provides an especially striking example of how the Grimms practically destroyed the whole point of a story in their zeal to render it less offensive to sensibilities which expected the [tales] to be above all charming, and never threatening. The manuscript tale—its basic elements still largely preserved in the first edition, though disturbed as early as the second edition—is the story of ambivalence in a relationship between mother and daughter. A woman wishes for a daughter of great beauty—a narcissistic wish on the part of a woman herself celebrated for her beauty. But when she gets her wish the mother realizes too late that this is not simply the further extension of her own beauty which her narcissistic wish had contemplated, but instead a separate person whose beauty rivals and eventually outdoes her own. Seeing what a dangerous threat she has invoked, the mother tries to destroy the daughter and, when she fails, is eventually destroyed by her. Now here is a dramatic version of mother-daughter rivalry and sexual jealousy, in which an older woman, at first identifying with the flesh of her flesh, later sees herself eclipsed by a younger woman who really is a separate person and thus a rival. The daughter's active participation in the rivalry is more than hinted at; for it is at her wedding—the celebration of her the ideal "Märchenfrau" by the Grimms: old, peasant, and Hessen. This slight woman, whose admirable recital Wilhelm described in his introduction to the second volume of the *Household Tales*, was introduced to the brothers probably around 1812 by the daughters of a clergyman. The young ladies often treated her to a bowl of soup or coffee in exchange for stories when she came by twice a week to sell them eggs and butter. At their urging, the story lady also visited the Grimms at their Kassel home and was treated generously by them. During their brief acquaintance (she died in 1815), Mrs. Viehmann told the brothers twenty-one new

own beauty and sexuality—that her mother is put to death in grisly fashion, being forced to dance in red-hot shoes until she drops dead. Thus, she is destroyed at the very celebration of her daughter's sexual power.

This is certainly a provocative story—fascinating study of the way in which a child begins its life as a narcissistic extension of its parent, and in growing up becomes a separate human being with all the problems that that entails. But in the second edition of this tale the Grimms introduced a key sentence which destroyed its meaning. After the sentence announcing the birth of the child the queen had wished for—as beautiful as she had wished—the text now adds: "When the child was born, the queen died. A year later, the king took another wife, but she was a beautiful woman, but proud of her beauty and could not bear the fact that anyone might surpass her in that."

In this version the woman who wishes for a beautiful daughter and gets her is *not* the same woman who envies her beauty or who is destroyed at her wedding; gone is the *ambivalence* of the battle of the generations, and the crucial link between the mother's narcissistic wish and its later results. The Grimms shrank from the real conflict between parents and children which derives from the children's growing up and becoming separate people. In the stage of conflict they substituted a stranger for the parent, and this softening of the impact of the tale removes its real interest. Now the tale has become one about the vanity of a specific person—it is not any longer a symbolic fantasy on the nature of a wish for a child and the danger of the fulfillment of that wish.

John M. Ellis, *One Fairy Story Too Many: The Brothers Grimm and Their Tales,* 1983.

tales and several variants of already known pieces. Among the stories of the "Viehmännin" were the "Lazy Spinning Girl," "The Girl Without Hands," "Dr. Know-It-All," "Hans My Hedgehog," "The Clever Peasant Girl," "The Poor Miller's Servant and the Cat," and "The Devil and his Grandmother." While she spoke, brother Ludwig Grimm made a portrait of her. The etching shows her kindly face, so characteristic of storytellers, and her worn hands. But she was by no means a peasant woman. As the widow of a tailor, she belonged to the urban middle class. Like the Grimms' hometown friends, she had no roots in Hessen either. As [German Folklorist] Rölleke has pointed out, she came "directly from a French Huguenot family and was raised in the French language so that her tale repertoire stemmed much more specifically from the stories of Perrault and d'Aulnoy than from the Hessen traditions." . . .

Evidently, the Grimms' recorded tales seldom, if ever, came originally "from the lips of the German folk." Narrators retold stories from the fashionable literary collections of [French writers] Aulnoy, Perrault, and others. Even tales from early German sources were selected for inclusion: the exemplum books and jestbooks of Montanus (one of the most popular Märchen, "The Brave Little Tailor," came from him), Johannes Pauli, Prätorius, Hans Sachs, and Froschmäuseler, among others.

The first seventy tales, largely from Hessen (but only few from Hessen ancestry), were published in the first volume of 1812. The rest (from different parts of the German-speaking territory, including Austria, Moravia, and Switzerland, and passed on to the Grimms by further fellow folk romantics) appeared in 1819 for the first time. A third volume in 1822 included scholarly comments and annotations.

GRIMMS AND THE BEGINNING OF FOLKLORE

The Grimm brothers were primarily scholars—linguists, historians of religion and literature, and students of customary law. Although their nationalistic vocation was obvious, the comparative method they initiated opened a new chapter in philology. They established a new discipline: the science of folklore. Their example of collecting oral literature launched general fieldwork in most European countries and resulted in the cooperative scholarly study of their prime focus of interest: the Märchen.

The *Household Tales* had set the model which was followed in similar basic collections by patriots of many European nations. Among others, Afanasiev collected in Russia, Asbjørnsen in Norway, Erben in Bohemia, Kolberg in Poland, Gaál in Hungary, Hahn in Greece and Albania. Scholars in different countries, driven by similar goals, produced evidence which disproved the claim of the Grimms that the tales were invented by the Germans and only borrowed by other races. *The Household Tales* soon became the standard work for international tale study, basic for comparative analysis. After [more than] a century and a half, they are still the target of research and remain an inexhaustible source of inspiration for tale scholarship.

Evidently, *Household Tales* was originally intended for the scholarly reader. Only under the pressures of success and popular demand did the Grimms turn more and more to the audience of children. As early as 1823, they published a selection of fifty illustrated tales which sold at a reasonable price and became the source of thousands of children's storybooks at home and abroad.

GRIMMS' EDITING PRACTICES

For fifty years, the brothers kept improving their texts. However, since Jacob's scholarly intentions had been carried out at the time of the first recordings, the published versions increasingly showed the stylistic editing of Wilhelm. The brothers were in agreement over the interpretation of the meaning of "authenticity": "truth and faithfulness to the folktext." Both Jacob, the scholar, and Wilhelm, the sensitive poet, felt that folktales were not so much the original creations of individuals whom they consulted but rather those of the "communal folk genius." Therefore, the *contents* must not be changed, but the awkward *wording* of the informants had to be modified. The editing amounted to an inspired rewriting of the heterogeneous body of narratives according to a standardized style. Although Jacob also reworked texts . . . it was Wilhelm's work to create a literary Märchen style which influenced both the oral and the written tale language in Germany and elsewhere. He did not work entirely on his own. The story of the "Juniper Tree" and "The Fisher and his Wife," collected from Pomeranian fishermen by painter Phillip Runge, served as models.

While the contents of the Grimm stories were scrupulously maintained, stylistic editing produced radical changes. It consisted of the embellishment and elaboration of details to a great extent, the polishing of rough edges, the correction of obvious errors, the replacement of indirect with direct speech, the addition of originally nonexistent dialogues, the addition of opening and closing as well as episode-connecting formulas and repetitions, the omission of subordinate clauses, transposition, and the equal distribution of dialect words and folk sayings. In many cases, the Grimms composed one perfect tale out of several less complete variants told by informants from different parts of Germany. The technique of editing and the improvement of the texts in the Grimm workshop can easily be followed by comparing the versions in the different editions. The following sample phrase from the "Briar Rose" [Sleeping Beauty] shows the nature of the elaboration:

The original [folktale] as written down by Jacob before 1810:

> . . . at the moment the king and his court returned, so began everything, everything in the castle to fall asleep, down to the flies on the wall. . . .

The 1812 version of the same phrase by Wilhelm:

> The king and queen had just come home, and when they entered the great hall they fell asleep and the whole court with them. The horses fell asleep in the stables, the dogs in the courtyard, the pigeons on the roof, and the flies on the wall, even the fire in the hearth stopped flaming and fell asleep, and the roast stopped cracking and the cook, who was about to pull the kitchen boy's hair because he had done something wrong, let go and fell asleep. And the kitchen maid let the cock which she plucked drop and went to sleep. . . .

The last sentence further extended in the 1819 edition:

> . . . and the wind died down, and not a leaf stirred on the tree outside the castle. . . .

Thus standardized, the *Household Tales* reflects a unity in narrative tone. This unity, however, does not change the fact that the collection itself is not composed of tales only. It is greatly diversified in terms of the origin, form, genre, function, and meaning of the stories. Many do not end happily at all and do not satisfy the expectations of the Märchen reader.

TALES MEANT FOR A DIVERSE AUDIENCE

On the basis of a comparative inventory of the Grimm collection by [*German folklorists*] Johannes Bolte and Georg Polívka, one can easily distinguish the following kinds of narratives: magic tales, about the miraculous career of lowly heroes and heroines; romantic love and adventure stories (novellas); Christian legends and miracle stories; didactic exempla; explanatory and origin legends; ghost stories; legends about evil spirits, witches, and the malevolent dead; fables; chain and catch tales; lying tales; and humorous anecdotes about numbskulls, tricksters, and adulterers.

This diversity has prompted folklorists to avoid the use of the term "Märchen" as an umbrella reference to the collection; some prefer to speak about the "Gattung Grimm" [the Grimm type]. At any rate, the romanticists who liked to consider this representative corpus of international folk narratives as comparable to the fashionable, reworked, pseudonaive literary "fairy tale" collections of the seventeenth and eighteenth centuries, were clearly mistaken. In terms of content, all of the tales were known in traditional peasant communities and were enjoyed by different age, sex, and occupational groups. Magic tales and novellas were told at adult get-togethers with the strict exclusion of children, as were most of the scary legends, exempla, and the spicy, realistic anecdotes. Women at late evening communal works exchanged ghost and horror stories along with funny anecdotes. Many female heroine-stories were popular with the girls busy with spinning: they enjoyed didactic and entertaining stories about lazy and ignorant girls as well as about lucky girls who marry a prince. Narratives for other occupational groups—craftsmen, farmhands, soldiers—were also represented in the Grimm repertoire. So were the narratives for young children.

But it is quite remarkable how little there is in this rich treasury for mothers and nurses actually to select for the bedtime entertainment of youngsters. Of course, there are the animal tales with sound imitation, the rhythmic catch tales, and the long, winding chain tales so popular with little children. Some of the simple religious legends are also appropriate. The story ladies must have had a difficult time following the advice of the Grimms and deciding what would be best for the children. All in all, the Bolte-Polívka catalog lists eighteen titles as children's stories. This makes a total of less than ten percent of the collection.

In addition, folklore scholars have recognized that one special set of stories, so-called scare and warning tales, are meant for children. Tales such as "The Wolf and the Seven Young Kids," "Hansel and Gretel," and "Red Riding Hood" are considered to be educational. In these, children are exposed to hostile powers without the protection of adults. Young listeners can learn how dangerous it is to open the door for strangers or to go along with them.

APPROPRIATE FOR CHILDREN?

This is exactly why, even before the publication of the *Tales*, the controversy mentioned earlier focused on this question: are Märchen actually "educational" for children or not? Are they beneficial or harmful to the young? Prior to the Grimms, oral tales in their natural state were regarded by the urban upper class intellectuals as silly lies, spreading superstitions and sheer irrationality, fit for drunken soldiers, spinning girls, old wives, and children. To elevate their status, to capture the attention of the educated audience, the tales required creative rewriting. According to the poet Wieland, "Nursery tales in the nurse's tone may spread through oral transmission but must not be printed. . . ." The suggestion of Wilhelm Grimm, that "These stories are pervaded by the same purity that makes children appear so marvelous and blessed to us," is convincingly interpreted by Alfred and Mary Elizabeth David: "It is not that the stories are primarily *for* children. . . , but the stories are *like* children, have lived *among* children, and have been treasured and preserved within the family. This childlike sense of wonder and the moral simplicity [are what] . . . the Grimms saw in fairy tales. . . ."

Friends and associates of the Grimm brothers expressed their concern over the exposure of children to the *Household Tales*. Achim von Arnim, among others, suggested that a subtitle should warn parents to exercise sound judgment in selecting stories for retelling. (In today's wording, we might say that he gave a "P.G." rating to the book.) The brothers took the advice to heart, but instead of adding a subtitle, included in the Introduction their suggestion of "parental guidance." They expressed the view that the tales represent pure poetry of great national value. Tales give pleasure and delight; therefore the collection would be a useful textbook for the education of children, if administered wisely and appropriately to the different age categories.

The pedagogical principles of the Grimms and their contemporaries, as shown in the use of tales, were rather limited. Their prime concern was the protection of children from vulgarities, rough language, and blasphemous expressions. They eliminated archaisms difficult to understand, as Arnim suggested, but felt that cruelties—for example, children play-butchering each other and parents eating their children—should not be omitted because such incidents were inherent in folk tradition. In an age when fright was regarded as the most effective disciplinary measure, it was necessary to keep children well-behaved, quiet, at home, and out of trouble. Child-devouring witches and ogres that lurked in the forest came in handy and were at the same time pedagogically acceptable, especially if conveyed through the poetic language of the tale.

An Ideological Tool

Having thus eliminated possible worries, those who judged the tales viewed them in a positive light for a long time—not only because of their educational value, but also because of their gratifying conclusion that permits all good people to "live happily ever after." The just outcome of the struggle between recognized good and evil powers was what mattered, regardless of the frightening, cruel, gory details or other potentially harmful elements.

The tremendous success of the Grimm storybook, writes [German Folklorist] Ingeborg Weber-Kellermann, cannot be explained only by its artistry. Socio-historic conditions—the aspirations of the German urban upper middle class family in the nineteenth century—were responsible for making the *Household Tales* an educational textbook to be read by mothers, grandmothers, and children alike. The harmonious whole, created from scraps of accidentally found traditional materials, fitted scientific and subjective tastes and gave an ideology for German nationalism and folk romanticism.

Hans Christian Andersen

Sven H. Rossel

"The Ugly Duckling," "The Little Mermaid," and "The Snow Queen" are amongst Hans Christian Andersen's most loved tales. In the following extract, Sven H. Rossel traces the evolution of Andersen's fairy tales from early folklore influences through the strong autobiographical and philosophical content of his later work. Themes range from triumph of the good heart over cold reason, to the absurdity of all human effort in the face of overwhelming odds. Andersen broke with the literary convention of the day, and through his extraordinary imagination, keen powers of observation, and identification with the social outcast, he made a unique contribution to the emerging literary fairy tale. Sven H. Rossel is Professor of Scandinavian Languages at Washington University in Seattle. Rossel's most recent work includes a book on Andersen's Diaries.

When, at the age of fourteen, Hans Christian Andersen left home to seek his fortune in the big city, his worried mother exclaimed, "Whatever will become of you?" He confidently replied, "I shall become famous." Years later, in his autobiography, *The Fairy Tale of My Life* (1855), experience led him to say it this way: "First you go through an awful lot, and then you become famous." Single-minded in pursuit of art and recognition, Andersen as a child of the working class, with only a rudimentary education and no social connections, had even more to go through than most struggling young artists. His conviction that he had been gifted at birth with extraordinary talent, however, saw him through much. As he says in "The Ugly Duckling": "It doesn't matter if one is born in a duck yard, when one has lain in a swan's egg!"

Andersen was the first prominent Danish writer of proletarian origin. Although he moved in bourgeois and aristocratic circles—in his day this was the only way for a writer to gain recognition and support—he never disguised his background but always considered himself an outsider and kept a sharp eye for the shortcomings of the bourgeoisie and aristocracy. In tales such as "The Nightingale" and "The Gardener and the Lord and Lady" Andersen's biting satire is aimed at the arrogance and selfishness of the aristocracy and court circles. Royalty itself, however, he places above criticism: when the nightingale says of the emperor of China, "I love your heart better than your crown," it continues, "and yet your crown has a scent of sanctity about it." Thus, Andersen did not become a great social writer like Charles Dickens, whose background was similar to that of his Danish friend and contemporary.

EARLY INFLUENCES AND EARLY TALES

As a child Andersen had heard retellings of old stories and tales; his father had read the *Arabian Nights* to him, and later he had become acquainted not only with the German Romantic literary tale as written by Ludwig Tieck, E.T.A. Hoffmann, and Adelbert von Chamisso, but also with the folktales collected by the Grimm brothers and with Mathias Winther's *Danish Folktales* (1823). All these sources are reflected in the first collection of tales in 1835, of which the first three are retold folktales. The fourth and weakest tale, "Little Ida's Flowers," is Andersen's own invention, but still dependent on a tale by Hoffmann, *Nutcracker and Mouseking* (1819). The discovery of the folktale became the chief element in Andersen's search for artistic independence. Here he found what he had previously lacked, the short form and firm structure. Here he found the technique of retelling the same episode three times—often with increasing effect—as in "The Tinderbox" (1835), "The Traveling Companion" (1835), and "Clod-Hans" (1855). As in the folktale, so in Andersen's tales there is usually only one main character, and all antagonists of this hero or heroine play subordinate roles. The main character suffers hardship, but usually Andersen's tales, especially those based directly on folktales, have a happy ending.

The first six collections of tales were subtitled "Told for Children." Andersen's statement that he had written them

exactly as he had heard them as a child reveals his ingenious discovery that the tales and stories have to be *told.*
Andersen's tales seem so simple, but the manuscripts tell
of all his patient labor to find the exact expression that
would fit his intention. He read recently finished tales and
stories to friends to find out if the words would fall as they
should and to register the reactions of his listeners. By
1844 Andersen had dropped the subtitle. He began to write
tales of greater length, and the three collections of
1852–55 bear the title "Stories." They contained such different texts as the science fiction fantasy "In a Thousand
Years' Time" and the social commentary "She Was No
Good." But Andersen did not give up the tale, and the last
eleven volumes—from 1858 on—bear the title "Tales and
Stories."

Andersen's early tales vary greatly in quality. In fact,
only a third of the 156 tales and stories represent him at
his best, and most of these date from the 1840s. "The
Nightingale," "The Sweethearts," and "The Ugly Duckling"
appeared in 1844; three of the finest tales, "The Snow
Queen," "The Fir Tree," and "The Bell" in 1845; "The Little Match Girl" in 1846; "The Shadow," "The Drop of Water," and "The Story of a Mother" in 1847. As a whole, the
production after 1850 does not reach the quality of the
masterpieces from the preceding decade. However, we still
find some excellent though less known texts, such as "In a
Thousand Years' Time" (1852), "She Was No Good" (1853),
"The Old Oak Tree's Last Dream" (1858), "The Butterfly"
(1861), "The Snail and the Rosebush" (1862), "What
People Do Think Up" (1869), "The Gardener and the Lord
and Lady," "The Cripple," and "Auntie Toothache" (1872).

AUTOBIOGRAPHICAL CONTENT OF FAIRY TALES

In his fragmentary but valuable comments on the tales
printed in the collected editions of 1862–63 and 1870–74, Andersen continually emphasizes the reality behind his imaginative treatment. He once stated: "Most of what I have written is a reflection of myself. Every character is taken from
life. I know and have known them all." In "The Ugly Duckling" we find the glorification of the author's own genius,
whereas "The Fir Tree" is a rather harsh judgment of himself
as the ambitious, always discontented artist afraid of having
passed his prime. Idealized reminiscences of Andersen's

childhood can be found in the opening of "The Snow Queen." We see self-portraits in the fortune-hunting soldier of "The Tinderbox" and the hypersensitive title character of "The Princess on the Pea." Andersen's affairs of the heart can be followed in several tales: "The Sweethearts" describes a meeting with Riborg Voigt thirteen years after his unsuccessful courtship; Louise Collin [daughter of patron, Jonas Collin] is probably the model for the proud princess in "The Swineherd," in which the swineherd, who turns out to be a prince, is Andersen himself; "The Nightingale" in its contrasting of the real and the artificial is a tribute to Jenny Lind [Swedish soprano who refused his proposal of marriage]; finally, he deals with his resignation to lonely bachelorhood in the witty parable "The Butterfly." Portraits of friends and acquaintances can also be found. It has been suggested that the prince in "The Bell" is Hans Christian Ørsted, the loyal friend who praised Andersen's first tales and who was also the discoverer of electromagnetism: in "The Bell" the prince represents the scientific mode of approaching the Divine, while the poor boy, another self-portrait of Andersen, represents the poetic mode. It has also been posited that the poet in "The Shadow" represents Andersen, and the title character has the features of Edvard Collin, just as in "The Ugly Duckling" the cat, the hen, and the old woman portray the Collin family. Andersen also carried on literary combat in his tales. It has been suggested that "The Snail and the Rosebush" is another reply to [Danish philosopher Soren] Kierkegaard's harsh criticism of *Only a Fiddler* (the snail, of course, is the philosopher, while the blooming rosebush is the poet himself), and "The Gardener and the Lord and Lady" is regarded as Andersen's final and wittiest settlement with his Danish critics.

PHILOSOPHICAL CONTENT

But the tales are more than disguised autobiographies and more than simple entertainment. "I seize an idea for older people—and then tell it to the young ones, while remembering that father and mother are listening and must have something to think about," Andersen says. "I write about what is true and good and beautiful," says the learned man in "The Shadow," stating Andersen's own ideal of art, which reflects the Romantic philosophy of his time. But the bitter irony of "The Shadow" is that everyone disregards the learned man and his values, choosing to follow the title figure, undoubtedly the most demonic character in Andersen's writings. By the end of the story there is nothing left of the Romantic belief that the goodhearted person, such as John in "The Traveling Companion" or Gerda in "The Snow Queen," has nothing to fear from evil: all human efforts are absurd. This is also the main theme of the tale "The Story of a Mother," a tribute to maternal love but also a demonstration of the mercilessness of life. Here we are far from the light gaiety of "The Tinderbox" or the optimism of "The Ugly Duckling."

OPTIMISM AND PESSIMISM

It is characteristic of Andersen's tales and stories that one idea evokes its counterpart, and this duality in his mental and spiritual make-up is recognizable in all his works. The tales deal with optimism *and* pessimism. In opposition to those which posit a belief in good fortune ("The Tinderbox," "The Traveling Companion," "The Flax," "Clod-Hans"), in the power of goodness of heart over cold reason ("The Snow Queen"), and in the possibility of human experience of the Divine ("The Bell"), we can cite many tales that are hopeless in their pessimism: "The Fir Tree," "The Shadow," "The Little Match Girl," "The Story of a Mother," and "Auntie Toothache." Thus Andersen's intense love of life alternates with a preoccupation with death: unable to accept the course of nature, he continually emphasizes immortality and fights death, as the mother does in "The Story of a Mother" and art does in "The Nightingale." The complete absorption in life as represented by the tiny mayfly in "The Old Oak Tree's Last Dream" remained Andersen's ideal.

But when Andersen aimed his satire at various inequalities in society, he never vacillated. Thus "The Nightingale" and "The Swineherd" should not only be interpreted as allegories, setting true poetry against rigid academic convention, but also as highly ironic depictions of human behavior, a critical tendency which is carried further in the social accusations in "The Drop of Water" and " 'She Was No Good.' "

REVIVING THE LITERARY FAIRY TALE

Andersen was no romantic dreamer with contempt for his own times. On the contrary, he welcomed many new events in art and science. He fantasizes about aircraft in "In a

Thousand Years' Time" and about a magnifying glass in "The Drop of Water." What he welcomed was the victory of spirit over matter, and he was interested in every new discovery that seemed to represent that victory. His own contribution along these lines was the renewing of the genre of the literary tale: "The tale is the most extensive realm of poetry, ranging from the blood-drenched graves of the past to the pious legends of a child's picture book, absorbing folk literature and art literature; to me it is the representation of all poetry, and the one who masters it must be able to put into it the tragic, the comic, the naïve, irony and humor, having here the lyrical note as well as the childish narrative and the language of describing nature at his service."

If Andersen himself was able to fulfill these, his own, demands, it was primarily because he, in contrast to the German Romanticists, was able to preserve that primitive immediacy that establishes direct contact with the world around him. His myth-creating imagination, which broke with all literary conventions, knew how to animate the inanimate. His acute power of observation and strong sense of reality endowed the most fantastic beings with realistic traits, forcing the reader to believe in them. Andersen's point of departure is local, Danish—yet his tales and stories live on, even though their creator has long since died.

"Will all beauty in the world die when you die?" the little fly asks the tree. "It will last longer, infinitely longer, than I can imagine!" says the great oak tree.

Frank Stockton, American Pioneer of Fairy Tales

Jack Zipes

Frank Stockton (1834–1902) is considered the first significant American writer of fairy tales. The values, content and themes of his stories are representative of early American writers of the genre, which differed substantially from their European counterpart. Stockton's fairy tales suggested that people could determine their own happiness by challenging abuses of authority, valuing contentment over riches, and transforming personal weaknesses into strengths. In her critical work *Down the Rabbit Hole,* Selma Lanes put it this way: "No glass slippers needed, thank you, and no fairy godmothers. Fairy tales were consolations for lives in need of magical solutions; but here man was master of his own fate."

Jack Zipes, Professor of German at the University of Minnesota, wrote the following article as an afterword to *The Fairy Tales of Frank Stockton* (1990). Among the foremost American writers on the sociohistorical approach to fairy tales, Zipes's publications include *Fairy Tales and the Art of Subversion* and *Don't Bet on the Prince: Contemporary Feminist Fairy Tales in North America and England.*

Although he wrote some of the most innovative fairy tales of the nineteenth century and was the first significant American writer of this genre, Stockton is hardly known today. This is not to say that he has fallen into total oblivion. During the 1960s an anthology of his stories, *A Story-Teller's Pack* (1968), was published, and three of his best fairy tales, *The Griffin and the Minor Canon* (1963), *The Bee-Man of Orn*

(1964), and *Old Pipes and the Dryad* (1968) were illustrated by such gifted artists as Maurice Sendak and Catherine Hanley. Yet, these publications represent only a small part of the achievement of Frank Stockton as a writer of fairy tales. In fact, during his lifetime he was regarded as one of America's most popular novelists and held in high esteem due to his unusual works of fantasy.

STOCKTON'S EARLY LIFE

Born on April 5, 1834 in Philadelphia, Stockton was the oldest of three sons in his father's second marriage to Emily Drean. His father, William, was one of the leading Methodists of his time and superintendent of the Alms House in Philadelphia when Frank was born. A severe and ascetic man, William, old enough to be his son's grandfather, was too busy conducting the affairs of the Alms House and writing religious tracts to supervise Frank's education. Consequently, his much younger wife, who was more open-minded, took charge of Frank's upbringing and gave him a good deal of freedom during his youth. Though partially lame from birth, Stockton enjoyed playing pranks, formed secret societies with his brothers, and read all kinds of fiction that his father condemned as scurrilous and decadent.

In 1844, Stockton and his brothers had to curtail their customary play at home when their father was dismissed as superintendent of the Alms House due to a minor financial scandal. The home was then turned into a sanctuary, where his father demanded a quiet atmosphere in order to write various religious books and speeches. Furthermore, his mother had less time to devote to him and his brothers since she founded a school for young ladies in West Philadelphia to help supplement the family income. By 1848, Stockton enrolled at Central High School, which had an outstanding curriculum in the sciences and arts, equivalent to some small colleges today, and he developed a strong interest in writing and the arts, often inventing and memorizing stories on his way to and from school. In a recollection written later in life he commented: "I was very young when I determined to write some fairy tales because my mind was full of them. I set to work, and in course of time, produced several which were printed. These were constructed according to my own ideas. I caused the fanciful creatures who inhabited the world of fairy-land to act, as far as possible for them to do so, as if they were inhabitants of the real world. I did not dispense with monsters and enchanters, or talking beasts and birds, but I obliged these creatures to infuse into their extraordinary actions a certain leaven of common sense."

STOCKTON'S WRITING CAREER

Despite his apparent literary proclivities, Stockton had to reach a compromise with his father, who was against his choosing a career as a writer, after graduation from high school in 1852: He decided to learn the trade of wood engraving, which would keep him in close contact with the

TRAITS OF AMERICAN FAIRY TALES

In her introductory article to American Fairy Tales, *Alison Lurie, Professor of American Literature from Cornell University, says that American fairy tales have always had a different underlying message from their European counterparts.*

The standard European fairy tale takes place in a fixed social world. In the usual plot a poor boy or girl, through some combination of luck, courage, beauty, kindness, and supernatural help, becomes rich or marries into royalty. In a variation, a prince or princess who has fallen under an evil enchantment, or been cast out by a cruel relative, regains his or her rightful position. In both types of story the social system is unquestioned and remains unchanged. What the characters hope for is to succeed within the terms of this system.

What makes American fairy tales unique is that in the most interesting of them this does not happen. Instead, the world within the story alters or is abandoned. Rip Van Winkle falls into a twenty-year sleep and wakes to find that a British colony has become a new nation in which "the very character of the people seemed changed." A hundred years later, the family in Carl Sandburg's story repeats the experience of many nineteenth-century immigrants and Western settlers. They sell all their possessions and ride to "where the railroad tracks run off into the sky"—to Rootabaga Country, which is not a fairy kingdom but rich farming country named after a large turnip.

In American fairy tales, even if the world does not change, its values are often implicitly criticized. The traditional European tales, though full of wicked stepmothers and cruel kings and queens, seldom attack the institutions of marriage or monarchy. They assume that what the heroine or hero wants is to become rich and marry well—if possible, into royalty.

arts and literature. From 1852 to 1860 Stockton had moderate success as a wood engraver, and he participated actively in the cultural affairs of the city. Aside from joining the Forensic and Literary Circle, a club in which various social issues were debated, he began submitting stories to publishers. After numerous rejections, his first short story "The Slight Mistake" was printed in the *American Courier*, but it was not until his next story, "Kate," published by the prestigious *Southern Literary Messenger* in December 1859, that Stockton gained the confidence he needed to pursue his writing career in a more active way.

Although a few American tales follow this convention, many do not. The guests who visit "The Rich Man's Place," in Horace Scudder's story, enjoy the palatial house and grounds but don't express a desire to live there. In Frank Stockton's "The Bee-man of Orn," a Junior Sorcerer discovers that an old beekeeper has been "transformed" from his original shape, and sets out to dissolve the enchantment. But as it turns out, the Bee-man's original shape (like everyone's) was that of a baby. Although the Junior Sorcerer restores him to infancy, when he grows up he does not become a prince, but a beekeeper again—and, as before, he is perfectly contented.

In American fairy tales, there is often not much to be said for wealth and high position, or even good looks. The witch in Hawthorne's "Feathertop" turns a scarecrow into a fine gentleman and sends him out into the world, where he exposes the superficiality and snobbery of the well-to-do. In L. Frank Baum's "The Glass Dog," the poor glass-blower manages to marry a princess, but she "was very jealous of his beauty and led him a dog's life."

The implication of such stories is that an American does not need to become rich or "marry up" in order to be happy; in fact, one should avoid doing so if possible. Happiness is all around one already, as the boy in Laura Richards's "The Golden Windows" discovers: his farmhouse already has "windows of gold and diamond" when the setting sun shines on it. Today, when there is so much pressure on Americans to want fame, power, and expensive objects, to feel dissatisfied with themselves and their possessions, these American fairy tales still have something to tell us.

Alison Lurie, introduction to *American Fairy Tales*, edited by Neil Phillip, 1996.

In more ways than one, 1860 was the turning point in his life. In April of that year he married Mary Ann (Marian) Tuttle, who had been teaching at the West Philadelphia School for Young Ladies established by Stockton's mother. Soon thereafter the couple moved to Knightly, New Jersey, to be in commuting distance from New York, where Stockton opened an engraving office. Later that year, as if to signal the completion of Stockton's independence as a young man, his father died at the age of seventy-five. From this point on, with the support of his wife, Stockton was bent on establishing himself as a writer. He only continued in the engraving business just as long as he did not have the money to support himself and his wife as a writer.

STOCKTON'S FIRST FAIRY TALES

In 1867 he returned to Philadelphia to help the Stockton family out of a financial dilemma and to assist his brother, John, who had helped found the newspaper *The Philadelphia Morning Post*. Interestingly, it was just at this time that Stockton wrote and published his first fairy tale, "Ting-a-ling," in *The Riverside Magazine*. From a biographical viewpoint, there is a connection between the tiny fairy, Ting-a-ling, who graciously helps friends and people in need with enterprising acts, and Stockton himself, who willingly came to the aid of his family and energetically embarked on a career of writing both for his brother's newspaper and for other journals. Two more "Ting-a-ling" tales soon appeared in *Riverside,* and all three stories were collected and published as Stockton's first book in 1870. Years later he was to comment:

> My first book was a long time in growing. It came up like a plant by the wayside of ordinary avocation, putting forth a few leaves at a time; and when at last it budded, there was good reason to doubt whether or not it really would blossom. At length, though, it did blossom, in red, brown, green, and blue. It was a book for young people and was called *Ting-a-ling.* It was made up of fairy stories, and when these first went out, each by itself, to seek a place in the field of current literature, it was not at all certain that they would ever find such a place. The fairies who figured in these tales were not like ordinary fairies. They went, as it were, like strangers or foreigners, seeking admission in a realm where they were unknown and where their rights as residents were some time in being recognized.

From the very beginning, Stockton's fairy tales eschewed heavy didactic and Christian messages, prevalent in children's literature at that time. The hallmark of his tales was formed by their droll humor and inquisitive spirit that led to a questioning of the norms of American society. Encouraged by the success of his early fairy tales, Stockton joined the staff of a new magazine, *Hearth and Home,* in December 1868. He was the assistant to the editor, Mary Mapes Dodge, author of *Hans Brinker and the Silver Skates,* and contributed numerous fairy tales to this publication. Moreover, since the journal was not primarily for children, Stockton could write articles and stories for adults that led to the publication of his second book, *Roundabout Rambles* (1872), a collection of sixty-nine articles dealing with natural phenomena, geography, geology, insect life, and magical illusions. By 1874 his superb editorial work on *Hearth and Home* prompted Scribner's to offer him the position of assistant editor, again to Mrs. Dodge, of the new periodical for young people *St. Nicholas Magazine.* Stockton accepted, and since Mrs. Dodge was only required to appear in the New York office once a week, he became the virtual editor of the magazine, which quickly became the most significant journal for young readers in America. However, due to the pressure of the editorial work (Stockton contributed more than forty-four pieces to the *St. Nicholas*) and the impairment of his eyesight, he was compelled to resign his post in 1878.

STOCKTON'S POPULARITY

Since it was extremely painful for Stockton to read or write, his wife Marian became his amanuensis, and he managed to continue publishing stories and novels for young and old on a prolific scale during the 1880s when his reputation began to soar. Indeed, aside from the successful appearance of his first novel for adults, *Rudder Grange* in 1879, he published a fine collection of fairy tales: *The Floating Prince and Other Fairy Tales* (1881); his most famous short story "The Lady, or the Tiger?" (1882); three volumes of short stories, *The Transferred Ghost* (1884), *The Lady, or the Tiger?* (1884), and *The Story of Viteau* (1884); the popular novels *The Casting Away of Mrs. Lecks and Mrs. Aleshine* (1886) and *The Hundredth Man* (1887); and his best collections of fairy tales, *The Bee-Man of Orn and Other Fanciful Tales* (1887) and *The Queen's Museum* (1887).

The Stocktons traveled a great deal during the 1880s and 1890s to Europe, the Bahamas, and throughout America.

One purpose was to give Stockton's eyes a rest; another, to gather material for stories and novels. Their home during this time was near Morristown, New Jersey, and it was there that Stockton dictated most of his works to his wife or a professional secretary. From 1889 until his death in 1902, he ventured forth into the field of science fiction, utopian fantasy, and travel literature by publishing such works as *The Great War Syndicate* (1889), *The Adventures of Captain Horn* (1895), *The Associate Hermits* (1899), and *A Bicycle of Cathay* (1900), all of which were best-sellers during his time but are forgotten today. Toward the end of his life Stockton himself felt that he was becoming too quaint for the American public. Yet, he was not dismayed by the loss of attention. Like many of his fairy-tale protagonists, he learned to keep a level head in face of adversity and believed that his works would not lose their value. In fact, he was supervising the Shenandoah collected edition of his writings and finishing a new novel when he died of a cerebral hemorrhage on April 20, 1902, while attending a banquet at the National Academy of Sciences in Washington, D.C.

THEMES AND VALUES IN STOCKTON'S FAIRY TALES

Most of his fairy tales were written between 1868 and 1890 when few American authors were developing this genre. Though the majority of the tales were published in magazines for young people, Stockton did not write them expressly for children. In fact, aside from the "Ting-a-ling" series, he claimed that his tales were also for mature audiences, and he had published them in periodicals for young people because they were the only magazines that would print them at the time.

Clearly, Stockton's tales appeal to young and old audiences. They are gracefully written and possess a gentle humor that often conceals a deep concern with disturbing social issues. For instance, a good many of Stockton's tales were conceived at the close of the Civil War and reflect his abhorrence of war. His wife was a Southerner, and he objected to the way that the North was imposing its views on the South. Stockton was for a peaceful resolution of the conflict and thought it best to allow the South to secede from the Union. Consequently, in such tales as "Derido; or, The Giant's Quilt," "The Magical Music," and "The Accommodating Circumstance," Stockton draws allusions to social upheaval and portrays protagonists who refuse to engage in war. Moreover, Stockton's protagonists do not use violence to achieve their goals, unlike the heroes of traditional folk tales in which "might makes right" is a common theme. In fact, Stockton's tales all deal with the abuse of power, but instead of punishing the evil oppressors by executing them, his narratives expose their foibles and make them look ridiculous.

If there are lessons to be learned in Stockton's tales, they have little to do with dogma, nor are they imposed on the reader's sensibility. Like Mark Twain, a writer whom he greatly admired, Stockton criticized the materialism and greed of the gilded age, and the themes of his tales propose alternatives to what were becoming the American standards for measuring success based on competition and achievement. Rarely does a Stockton protagonist want to compete, and there are just as many unfulfilled quests as there are accomplished tasks. The Bee-Man of Orn sets out to become transformed only to change back into himself again. Loris and the Ninkum never reach the idyllic castle of Bim. The banished king resigns his post after learning that he was a bumbler. Gudra's daughter is educated by failing to obtain what her father wanted to obtain. The competition in "The Great Show in Kobol-Land" is undermined and war and revolution are avoided because Millice and Chamian refuse to compete as the evil Gromiline had hoped. "Failure" for Stockton meant coming to one's senses, as one can readily see in a tale like "The Sisters Three and the Kilmaree," in which a fairy teaches the prince, the expectant heir, and clever Terzan how to make *sober* use of their gifts and appreciate what they have before they can visit the three sisters.

TRAITS OF AMERICAN FAIRY TALES

Stockton's technique as a writer was to describe all conditions and scenes, no matter how fabulous, as realistically as possible and to turn the world upside down by introducing extraordinary events and characters in a matter-of-fact way. By blending the normal with the abnormal, Stockton could create probable situations in which questions about arbitrary actions could be raised. Perhaps it was due to his rebellion against the strictures of his father and the Methodist Church, or simply his dislike of crude force and the violation of human rights. Whatever the case may be, Stockton's major concern in his fairy tales was to reveal the ridiculous nature of commands, impositions, and laws that are not developed by the people themselves and do not make common sense. Thus in "The Queen's Museum," a stranger enables the queen to realize how foolish she had been to force her people to revere the objects in her museum. The prince in "The Floating Prince," who is thrown out of his kingdom, is able to establish a new one with the cooperation of an unusual assortment of people. The answer to the evil forces in Stockton's fairy tales is generally the exercise of kindness and compassion. In "Old Pipes and the Dryad" the shepherd is rewarded for his kindness to the dryad. The count in "The Poor Count's Christmas" is helped by the fairy and the giant because of his charitable ways. Selma in "The Emergency Princess" is given a gift of gold by the gnomes because she graciously agrees to raise the gnome prince. Of course, Stockton also depicted what would happen if people were ungrateful and, in his most "pessimistic" fairy tale, "The Griffin and the Minor Canon," which is similar to some of Twain's tales, he condemned the townspeople for their cowardice and selfishness and left his readers with a bleak picture of the future.

For the most part, however, Stockton's tales are optimistic and prepared the way for the next great writer of fairy tales and fantasy in America, L. Frank Baum, who began his Oz books about the time of Stockton's death. Indeed, Baum's creation of the Land of Oz, in which violence is deplored and compassion for others highly regarded, reflects a continuity with the major themes of Stockton's fairy tales. Both writers used fantasy to demonstrate how oppressed characters could resist force and form worlds in which they could determine a measure of their happiness. In particular, Stockton delighted in revealing how humans could transform their weaknesses and limitations into strengths, and the magical revelations of his fairy tales form the essence of their unusual appeal today.

CHAPTER 3

Analyzing Fairy Tales

Fairy
Tales

Characters and Characterization in "Beauty and the Beast"

Betsy Hearne

In *Beauty and the Beast: Visions and Revisions of an Old Tale*, Betsy Hearne traces the development of the famous tale from the first literary version by Madame de Beaumont in 1756 to the present day films and television series. In the following extract Hearne analyzes the central characters and themes of the fairy tale which do much to explain its enduring popularity. Recognition of the beautiful and brutal qualities in human nature, the possibility of being accepted and loved by another human being, and developing sympathy for one's own dark side are some of the themes she discusses. Betsy Hearne teaches Children's Literature and Storytelling at the University of Illinois in Urbana, Champaign and has been studying "Beauty and the Beast" tales for over twenty years.

Depending on how many characters are introduced, "Beauty and the Beast" can be a social drama, family drama, triangle, courtship, or lonely struggle for individual fulfillment. Beauty and the Beast are clearly essential, but at least one version . . . avoids their actual encounter by means of alternate monologues, stressing the rounding of each personality through implied contact with the other. Almost as important as Beauty and the Beast in most versions is the role of the family—Beauty's father and sisters—to which is often added the dream comforter or choral/adviser/mother figure. . . . The brothers and animal helpers are variable in both number and role.

All of the characters have a capacity for both symbolism and development, role function and relationship, which lends their appearances great flexibility. The father has been presented as weak or strong, with varying shades of complexity between. The siblings have been portrayed as anything from good to ungracious to villainous, Beauty from vacuous to determined, the chorus from sanctimonious to witty to wise, the animal helpers from mechanical to sympathetic. Whatever the degree of development, their symbolic nature is clear; yet without any development at all, their archetypal patterns are still satisfying.

ALIENATION, ISOLATION, RECONCILIATION

These patterns include the father-daughter relationship, sibling rivalry, courtship, the father-daughter-suitor triangle, and the chorus-protagonist-(reader) affiliation. In only three versions does the father have a relationship with anyone other than Beauty. . . . In none does Beauty have other contacts outside the family, chorus, and Beast. Her only friends are animal helpers, variously horses, birds, or dogs. The three main characters (Beauty, the Beast, and the father) who develop in the course of almost all versions, reflect, in their growth, the same kind of rhythmic movement apparent in the plot: *alienation, isolation, reconciliation.* This is identifiable as a basic pattern of internal growth by anyone faced with disrupting change. The father, alienated from his family after Beauty leaves, retreats into the isolation of illness before he can accept Beauty's coming of age and reconcile himself to old age.

Beauty herself clearly follows this pattern. Her visit home only clarifies an alienation she has long experienced. She is marked by difference; and more, she is changing. Her isolation at the palace is a vision quest, removed from time, a realization of maturing sexuality and spiritual growth. As [American folklorist] Joseph Campbell has declared of Psyche,[1] Beauty is the hero of the tale. This is even more true in Beauty's case than in Psyche's because Beauty is not thrown to her fate but chooses it, however reluctantly. Reluctance characterizes many of the heroes cited by Campbell—it is perhaps a sign of intelligence, given what lies ahead. Yet the hero must venture forth or live forever unfulfilled.

---

1. "Cupid and Psyche" is a folktale recorded by Roman writer Apulieus in the second century A.D. with marked similarities to "Beauty and the Beast."

Beauty's is the journey to the underworld, to existence beneath surface appearances. Along the way, she faces the danger all heroes encounter, a monster representing—perhaps created by—her own fear. Beauty's triumph is a strength of perception that leads to reconciliation with self, mate, family, and society. Her good looks become irrelevant, an ironic context for her previous failure to see. As her inner vision clears, she refocuses the old adage: beauty is in the eye of the beholder. Beauty is not what one sees but how one looks at it, not passively, artificially, but actively, probingly. Her vision becomes a "burning gaze." Beauty, like the Beast, is an inner force. In dissipating her fears, she dissipates the fearsome aspects of the Beast.

HUMBLING EXPERIENCES EXPOSE THE TRUE HEART

Because he is the catalyst for change, tension, and conclusion; pivotal to beginning, middle, and end; and the concentric focus in relationships with each and all the other characters, the Beast is the center of the story. Of the whole cast, it is the Beast who provides the unique and most compelling element of the tale, who offers both writers and illustrators the most imaginative possibilities for interpretation. This figure is presented with dimensions unusual to fairy tale males. Although one can point to plenty of handsome princes or even precedents for good-hearted blockheads who can make a princess laugh (surely a sensible prerequisite for marriage), those are barely outlined heroic or comic figures, while the Beast is fully sensitive and potentially tragic. He is, in short, capable of love, an emotion of little importance in the development of many fairy tales except as a convenient denouement. The Beast's courtship is never assumed or forced. At the beginning, he lures Beauty through her bonds of affection for her father but soon works to transfer them to himself. When she refuses his nightly proposals, he sadly retreats and tries again the next day. His redemption from loneliness depends, not on strength or valor, but on another's love and consent.

The Beast is neither a comic *dummling* nor a clever adventurer, and of course he is not handsome. He uses none of the traditional male accoutrements of power and daring; what he does is set a good table and wait. In fact, he shows traditionally female attributes of delicate respect for Beauty's feelings, nurturance, comfort, gentleness, and patience, all of which he has learned through a humbling experience. He has learned the hard way that life without undeceived affection is rather a thorny paradise, even fenced with roses; Beauty must learn the same. To expose the true heart, Beast has been stripped of his beauty and wit, as Beauty loses her wealth, status, and family. By dint of such exposure and by the intimacy established between the characters and the reader, one is suddenly looking not only at another fairy tale time but also very close to home.

COMPASSION FOR THE BEAST WITHIN

The moment when Beauty faces the Beast is psychologically familiar and offers a barely concealed point of identification for the modern reader (it is precarious to speculate about earlier states of consciousness). Each person knows a moment of fear in beholding the beast in others or him/herself. On a deeper level, each knows the slow growth of loving and accepting the unacceptable, whereupon, miraculously, disparate parts become integrated. The fear of being unacceptable lies deep within child or adult reader. The bestial part may be hidden, yet is always present, tempting exposure, either by welling up from within (as portrayed in Cocteau's Beast hunting his prey at night) or by responding to the charisma of it in others. "Beauty and the Beast" offers the promise that for all our human ugliness and brutality, we can be acceptable, even lovable, to another human being.

The continuing relevance of "Beauty and the Beast" as a modern theme stems from this fearful knowledge that we are each beastly, juxtaposed with the hopeful knowledge that we are each beautiful. Moreover, whatever the imbalance of our inner beauty and beast, we seek to balance with others who have complementary imbalances. The story is a fundamental recognition and definition of what is "good and bad" in each individual and each relationship. The complexity of that good and bad includes but goes beyond the Freudian sexual interpretation commonly articulated in explanation of the story. Certainly the tale is sexual. Beauty's relationship with the Beast is, after all, a journey from fearful revulsion through platonic affection to the acceptance of a sexual mate, a husband. Her attachment to her father is devoted, almost erotic as described in their reunion, during which her father, responding to the maid's shriek at finding Beauty back home in bed, "held her fast locked in his arms above a quarter of an hour. As soon as the first transports were over, Beauty began to think of rising, and was afraid she had no clothes to put on. . . ."

Beauty learns to appreciate and finally takes the consummate mate. Yet outlining the transference of a child's oedipal attachment to acceptance of mature sexual love, while accurate, seems to disregard some other important aspects and leaves little room for the human variables of time and place that the story seems to encompass. That the "marriage of Beauty and the Beast is the humanization and socialization of the id by the superego," may very well be what [French author] Beaumont, in terms of her own society [eighteenth century France], intended by that final ecstatic transformation. Yet a reader's common response to the story is actual sympathy for, identification with, and attraction to the Beast, a brute force harnessed by need. The id seems to supersede the ego as the story's prime focus.

The transformed or tamed (read "humanized") prince is not nearly so memorable as the Beast, a figure of power and vulnerability combined. That is a rich combination of natures. It is the Beast as beast who rivets attention and burns the story into one's mind. It is the Beast on whom storytellers, writers, and artists focus their imaginations. The climax of the story is Beauty's love of the Beast himself, not the transformation and marriage, which is anticlimactic if pleasant. Therein lies the great disappointment of many graphic and literary conclusions of "Beauty and the Beast." The prince seems bland in contrast to the powerful reconciled beast; he is in fact anticlimactic to the forceful struggle of balancing beauty and beast. The final product must be not a handsome saint but a whole human being. The Beast has our sympathy already, and his is a hard act to follow.

"Little Red Riding Hood": Victim of the Revisers

Carole and D.T. Hanks Jr.

The original "Little Red Riding Hood" written by
Charles Perrault in 1697, differs substantially from
popular American versions of the fairy tale. In the
following article, Carole and D.T. Hanks Jr. show
how modern versions have robbed the original tale
of its powerful theme and central erotic metaphor.
"Mind your mother" and "you will be saved in the
end, despite your error" are greatly inferior messages to those of the true tale with its shocking ending and disturbing sense of injustice. Perrault's tale
suggests that beauty, goodness, and innocence can
be destroyed and that maturing is a risky business
because in the real world "the wolf awaits." Carole
and D.T. Hanks Jr. were members of the English De-
partment of Baylor University in Texas when they
wrote the article.

Charles Perrault's "*Le petit chaperon rouge*" is centered on an
erotic metaphor and ends tragically; yet neither of these elements of the tale figure in modern translations of the story.

Perrault's tale provides a classic example of the bowdler-
izing which all too often afflicts children's literature. Derived from the [Grimms'] version, "*Rotkäppchen*," American versions of the tale have been sanitized to the point
where the erotic element disappears and the tragic ending
becomes comic. This approach emasculates a powerful
story, one which unrevised is a metaphor for the maturing
process. It will be suggested, mostly between the lines, that
much of the considerable literary value of the tale disappears in the revisions.

Excerpted from "Perrault's 'Little Red Riding Hood': Victim of the Revisers," by Carole
and D.T. Hanks Jr., *Children's Literature*, 1978. Reprinted with permission from Carole
Hanks.

"*Le petit chaperon rouge*" is a brief tale composed of sixty-one lines of prose and a fifteen-line rhymed "*Moralité.*" The "moral" warns children, especially attractive young girls, against listening to all men *("toutes sortes de gens").* Some of them, seemingly gentle, are actually wolves.

"*Le petit chaperon rouge*" has been so popular since Perrault wrote it, that some folklorists have felt it must be part of the European oral tradition. Most students of the fairy tale, however, and some of the most eminent scholars of folklore, suggest that the tale originated with Perrault. Be that as it may, Perrault's tale is classic in its simplicity and finality.

LITTLE RED RIDING HOOD: A STORY

Once there was a little village girl, the prettiest that was ever seen. Her mother doted on her, and her grandmother doted still more. Indeed, this good woman made for her a little red hood which became her so well that everyone called her "Little Red Riding Hood."

One day her mother, having baked some shortcakes, said to Little Red Riding Hood, "Go see how your grandmother is feeling; someone told me that she was ill. Take her a shortcake and this little pot of butter." Little Red Riding Hood left immediately for the house of her grandmother, who lived in another village.

Entering into a wood, she met Sly Wolf, who very much wished to eat her but did not dare for fear of some woodcutters who were in the forest. He asked her where she was going; the poor child, who had not yet learned that it is dangerous to stop to listen to a wolf, said to him, "I am going to see my grandmother and take her a shortcake, along with a little pot of butter that my mother is sending her."

"Does she live very far away?" the wolf asked her.

"Oh, yes!" said Little Red Riding Hood. "It's by the mill which you see right over there; over there it's the first house in the village."

"Well now," said the wolf to her, "I want to go there and see her too. I will go by this road here, and you by that road there; we will see who will be there sooner."

The wolf began to run with all his strength along the shorter road, and the little girl walked on by the longer one, amusing herself by picking hazelnuts, running after butterflies, and making bouquets of the little flowers that she came across.

It was not long before the wolf arrived at the home of the grandmother. He knocked at her door, "toc, toc."

"Who's there?"

"It's your granddaughter, Little Red Riding Hood," said the wolf, disguising his voice. "I'm bringing you a shortcake along with a little pot of butter that my mother is sending you."

The good grandmother, who was in her bed because she felt slightly ill, called out, "Pull back the bolt, the latch will open."

The wolf pulled the bolt and the door opened; he threw himself upon the good woman immediately and consumed her in less than no time, for it had been three days since he had eaten.

Then he closed the door and lay down in the grandmother's bed to wait for Little Red Riding Hood. A moment later she came knocking at the door: "toc, toc."

"WHO'S THERE?"

Little Red Riding Hood, hearing the wolf's deep voice, was afraid at first. But, thinking that her grandmother must have a sore throat, she replied, "It's your granddaughter, Little Red Riding Hood; I'm bringing you a shortcake along with a little pot of butter that my mother is sending you."

The wolf called out, softening his voice a little, "Pull back the bolt, the latch will open."

Little Red Riding Hood pulled back the bolt and the door of the house opened. The wolf, seeing her enter, said from within the bed where he was concealing himself under the covers, "Put the shortcake and the little pot of butter on the cupboard and come to bed with me."

Little Red Riding Hood took off her clothes and went to get into the bed, where she was greatly astonished to see how her grandmother looked in her night clothes. She said, "Grandmother, what big arms you have!"

"The better to embrace you, my child," the wolf replied.

"Grandmother, what big legs you have!"

"The better to run, my child."

"Grandmother, what big ears you have!"

"The better to hear, my child."

"Grandmother, what big eyes you have!"

"The better to see, my child."

"Grandmother, what big teeth you have!"

"TO EAT YOU!" And saying these words, that wicked wolf threw himself on Little Red Riding Hood and ate her.

Moral
One sees here that young children,
And especially young girls
Who are pretty, well-formed, and pleasing,
Are wrong to listen to all sorts of men,
And that it is not a strange thing
That there are so many of them whom the wolf eats.
I say *the* wolf, because all wolves
Are not of the same kind;
Some of them have a pleasing air,
Not noisy, not sarcastic, not wrathful,
Are self-effacing, obliging, and pleasant,
Following the young ladies
Into dwellings as well as in the streets.
But alas! for her who does not know that these pleasant wolves
Are of all wolves the most dangerous.

The End

PROTOTYPES OF INNOCENCE AND MENACE

The tale's brevity makes it clear that Perrault is here uncon-cerned with character development or an elaborate plot. He establishes his protagonist in two sentences: she is a young village girl, the prettiest ever; her mother and grandmother dote on her; she wears a red cap, or hood, which the loving grandmother has made for her. After this point we learn only three more elements of the little girl's character: she is to make an independent journey away from her mother; she has not learned that it is dangerous to listen or talk to a wolf; and she enjoys hazelnuts, butterflies, and flowers. With these carefully-selected details Perrault sketches the proto-typical innocent little girl leaving the home. She is both beautiful and beloved, and customarily inhabits a secure and exclusively female world; she does not fear the Outsider, and she is identified with the natural beauties of nuts, flow-ers, and butterflies.

Perrault employs his other human characters simply as devices. They establish Little Red Riding Hood's lovable quality and provide the motivation for her journey. They are not otherwise important in the story, except of course as a grandmotherly *hors d'oeuvre.*

The wolf is the other major character. He is personified menace, and Perrault selects only the details necessary to establish his role in Little Red Riding Hood's world. His simply being a wolf is probably sufficient to support his menace, since wolves are widely slandered in European (and American) tradition. Perrault also introduces him as *"compere le Loup"* (Wolf, the deceiver) in his initial meeting with Little Red Riding Hood, and adds immediately that he "very much wished to eat" the little girl. The wolf is firmly established as the villain and as the only male in the story the working-out of the plot is inevitable.

Inevitable and classic. Given an innocent who has not learned to fear wolves, her initial deception is a matter of course, as is her final destruction. All that is necessary is for the two central characters to meet again, in surroundings where the wolf need not fear the intervention of woodcutters. Perrault brings the two together in just such circumstances in the grandmother's home. He then underscores the destructively treacherous nature of the wolf by having him engage in a metaphorical seduction: he tells Little Red Riding Hood to join him in bed and she does so, first disrobing. The stage is set and the major action of the tragedy is set in motion. Perrault brings about the dénoument, and reinforces the essential natures of wolf and little girl in his closing dialogue. This famous antiphon indicates the little girl's innocent wonder at her "grandmother's" size and, at the same time, re-establishes the wolfishness which that size actually manifests. All that is then required, or artistically appropriate, is to end dialogue and tale with:

> "Grandmother, what big teeth you have!"
> "TO EAT YOU!" And saying these words, the wicked wolf threw himself on Little Red Riding Hood and ate her.

THE THEME OF INNOCENCE DESTROYED

The tale's central metaphor and theme seem fairly clear. Perrault saw fit to underline them, nonetheless, in his closing *"Moralité"*: pretty young girls should not listen to "all sorts of men," he warns, lest they be devoured by *"le Loup."* Obviously, Perrault uses "the Wolf" as a metaphor, if not for "all sorts of men" at any rate for those whom he characterizes as quiet, self-effacing, anxious to please, and "the most dangerous."

This is not to say, however, that the tale is simply a metaphorical seduction—even though the wolf does indeed lure Little Red Riding Hood out of her clothes and into bed. Perrault wrought better than that, perhaps better than he knew. "Little Red Riding Hood" is the tale of the innocent who leaves home, meets the betrayer, doffs her family gift of warmth and protection (the [hood or] "chaperon"), and is destroyed. It is in a way the ultimate tragedy, if that is not too grandiose a term for a three-page fairy tale; youth and innocence leave home only to be destroyed guiltless. Something similar happened to Job's children.

FAIRY TALES AND FEAR

In Tremendous Trifles, *a collection of articles published in 1909, British Literary critic G.K. Chesterton included two chapters in defense of fairy tales. He said that fairy tales do not introduce children to the idea of evil, but rather provide them with the notion that there exists a fairy tale hero or heroine who can defeat that evil. In the following extract from "The Red Angel", Chesteron asserts that fear is not derived from fairy tales, but is part of the human condition.*

I find that there really are human beings who think fairy tales bad for children. . . . A lady has written me an earnest letter saying that fairy tales ought not to be taught to children even if they are true. She says that it is cruel to tell children fairy tales, because it frightens them. You might just as well say that it is cruel to give girls sentimental novels because it makes them cry. All this kind of talk is based on that complete forgetting of what a child is like which has been the firm foundation of so many educational schemes. If you kept bogies and goblins away from children they would make them up for themselves. One small child in the dark can invent more hells than Swedenborg. One small child can imagine monsters too big and black to get into any picture, and give them names too unearthly and cacophonous to have occurred in the cries of any lunatic. The child, to begin with, commonly likes horrors, and he continues to indulge in them even when he does not like them. There is just as much difficulty in saying exactly where pure pain begins in his case, as there is in ours when we walk of our own free will into the torture-chamber of a great tragedy. The fear does not come from fairy tales; the fear comes from the universe of the soul.

G.K. Chesterton, *Tremendous Trifles*, 1909.

Indeed, the basic theme of the tale is akin to that of *Job;* innocence, beauty, and goodness are destroyed by their opposites. In "Little Red Riding Hood" this theme is embodied in the tale of the child who leaves parent and home in order to engage in an independent action. The child commits no wrong, but the world of the forest deceives and destroys her. It is probably unnecessary to point out that such occurrences are facts of life. The continued popularity of Perrault's tale in France testifies to children's willing reception of the grim finality of the tale.

THEME REVERSED IN AMERICAN VERSIONS

That grim finality is almost entirely missing from American versions of the tale. Most of them—even those which attribute the story to Perrault—delete the erotic element, provide a "moral" absent from Perrault's story, and deliver Little Red Riding Hood and her grandmother unharmed from the depths of the wolf. In short, most American retellings of the tale transmute it to the version which the brothers Grimm published as Number 26 in their [tale] "*Rotkäppchen.*"

"*Rotkäppchen,*" ironically, appears to be derived from Perrault's tale rather than from the "oral tradition," as the Grimms believed. The tale suffered major revisions as it crossed the border; since the same revisions appear in most American versions, the important ones are presented here in some detail:

1. The mother's directions to *Rotkäppchen* in the Grimm story are quite detailed, and moreover provide the inception of the moral of the story: "walk along nicely and don't leave the path."

2. There are no woodcutters nearby when the wolf meets *Rotkäppchen,* but he spares her in order to later consume both the child and the grandmother. He tells himself, "You must manage this slyly, so that you can snap them both up."

3. The wolf tempts *Rotkäppchen* to delay in order to pick flowers and listen to the birds. She leaves the path in order to do so.

4. The erotic element vanishes; the wolf conceals himself in the bed, but *Rotkäppchen* begins her series of "Grandmother what big . . ." exclamations from alongside it, and the wolf leaps out of it to devour her.

5. The tale ends as comedy rather than tragedy. When the wolf has consumed both the grandmother and *Rotkäppchen,* he returns to the bed, sleeps, and snores. A passing hunts-man investigates the loud snoring and surgically rescues the women from the wolf's belly as the wolf sleeps on. They fill the resulting cavity with stones, the weight of which kills the wolf when he awakens and tries to spring up. Everyone is happy; the huntsman takes the wolf's pelt, the grandmother takes the cake and wine, and *Rotkäppchen* takes the moral, as she tells herself, "Never again in your life will you have a mind to leave the path to go off alone into the forest, when your mother has forbidden it to you."

These revisions "clean up" and reverse the theme of Perrault's tale. In the Grimm tale, the point is that some-one will always take care of the child—even if she steps off the path. There will always be someone there, and youth and innocence—having learnt its lesson—will be rescued unchanged, resolved henceforth to mind Mother. The re-vised tale denies that the child can leave home and find destruction—instead, its point is "Mind your mother."

Perrault's tale, on the other hand, points out that leaving home, becoming independent of the parent, is a risky un-dertaking. It may result in disaster, not through the child's fault but because that's the way the world is. Its point is, "The wolf awaits."

"The wolf awaits" is not a popular moral among American translators and publishers of *"Le petit . . ."* The overwhelm-ing majority of American editions of "Little Red Riding Hood" in our local library, in the University of Minnesota education library, and in the Kerlan collection of children's books at the University of Minnesota, repress the central erotic metaphor and replace the tragic ending with the Grimms' happy end-ing. This occurs even when the tale is attributed to Perrault.

In short, the American publishers of "Little Red Riding Hood" have protected their audience—our children—from the sexuality and violent death which Perrault built into his tale. They have revised away sex and death from a story which is a metaphoric rendering of the maturation process; they have denied the maturing process. Their heroine is res-cued by an obvious father figure, and she resolves never again to "step off the path" to disobey the mother. Her inde-pendent action is portrayed as an aberration which automatically receives punishment. Independence is bad. Dependence is good. Remain a child.

Perrault's tale does not urge the child to remain immature, nor does it urge the opposite. His tale takes it for granted that a child will mature, that it will leave the home and the parent to engage in an independent task. But Perrault's tale points out that maturing is risky; there *are* dangers in the forest—if the maturing person makes a misstep (not necessarily through any personal fault), then he or she may perish. It's unjust, of course—as Job pointed out long ago, yet it is a fact. It is an important fact for those who plan to grow up; we do our children a disservice by protecting them from it. We also provide them with an inferior literary experience. The shocking ending, the injustice of Perrault's tale hits home; it prompts us to think further about the story we have just read. The Grimm tale, on the other hand, has no such impact. We can relax as we finish it; disaster has been averted, huntsmen will always providentially pass by, and Little Red Riding Hood will not step off the path again.

Structure and Themes in "Snow White"

Steven Swann Jones

In the following article, Steven Swann Jones identifies the generic structure of "Snow White" by comparing German, Italian, and Asian versions of the
fairy tale. The structure, as Jones shows, is en-
twined with the style, theme, and dramatic tension
of the narrative. It also mirrors social rituals or
rites of passage of the heroine through life, which
underscores the function of the tale—to help
women cope with major life transitions as they
grow and mature. Steven Swann Jones is professor
of English at California State University, Los Angeles. The structure of "Snow White" was the subject
of his doctoral dissertation.

The generic structure of "Snow White" is a pattern of action underlying that narrative that reveals the essential
connection between "Snow White" and other related folktales of persecuted heroines as well as the fundamental relationship between these tales and the society from which
they grew. In *Morphology of the Folktale*, a classic work on
the structural approach to fairy tales, Russian folklorist
Vladimir Propp suggests that we can describe these generic
structures by identifying the tale's functions, the pattern of
basic events common to different stories. Specifically, the
fundamental pattern of action of "Snow White" and certain
related folktales of persecuted heroines depicts a repetition
of hostilities directed against the heroine. These hostilities
recur with increasingly serious consequences until the
drama is resolved. This succession of incremental hostilities may be considered the essential paradigm both of
"Snow White" and of other folktales of persecuted heroines, and it reveals an underlying connection between this
folktale and its audience.

Excerpted from "The Structure of 'Snow White,'" by Steven Swann Jones, *Fabula*, 1983.
Reprinted with permission from Walter de Gruyter Publishers.

In "Snow White," the cycle of hostilities directed against the heroine involves three steps: first, a threat is directed against the heroine; second, that threat is realized in some form of hostility; and finally, a rescue or escape from the hostility is effected. This cycle is generally repeated twice in the narrative of "Snow White": first, when she is initially threatened, expelled, and then adopted; and second, when she is attacked, killed, and finally resuscitated and married. Versions of "Snow White" follow this persecution pattern faithfully, presenting us generally with two instances or separate occasions of hostility directed against the heroine.

The evidence supporting the presence of a twofold repetition of a persecution cycle in "Snow White" is difficult to present in an abbreviated form, because we cannot review scores of versions in order to show the manifestation of the persecution pattern. However, we can summarize the general action of the story and show how the motifs from three sample versions illustrate the presence of the generic persecution pattern in "Snow White." Accordingly, in Table 1, I have outlined the generic pattern of actions (labeled "functions" after Propp's terminology) found in "Snow White." Furthermore, I have listed the corresponding episodes and motifs that illustrate the generic pattern outlined here. For reasons of familiarity, I have listed the motifs from the Grimm version, but by way of corroboration, I have included motifs from one version from Italy (recorded by Thomas Crane) and one from Asia Minor (recorded by Henry Carnoy).

STRUCTURAL REPETITION OF EVENTS

The way the episodes identified in Part 1 are essentially duplicated in Part 2 suggests the idea that a double pattern of hostility underlies in "Snow White." As we can see from Table 1, the events of the second half repeat more intensively the events in the first half of the story: once again the mother (persecutor) becomes jealous and tries to attack the heroine, but the heroine is ultimately rescued. In the beginning of both parts, a villainous figure contrives an intense dislike for the heroine in an initial threatening situation; then the persecutor becomes envious of the heroine and wishes to be rid of her, as we see in the motif of the magic mirror, in the motif of the breaking of plates and glasses, or in the motif of the boastful eagle. And accordingly, in both parts, a hostile action is subsequently initiated. In Part 1, as illustrated by the motifs in the table, the heroine is expelled or ordered to perform a dangerous chore or taken away to be killed, while in Part 2 the heroine is killed by the use of a poisoned stay-lace, comb, apple, ring, raisin, sweetmeat, or dress. Finally, in both parts, the heroine manages to escape from the hostility in a way that significantly alters her situation, status, and environment. In Part 1, she leaves home and finds a new home with her companions, while in Part 2, she leaves the companions' establishment for the home of her new husband. The crucial distinction that reveals the structural repetition of the generic pattern in "Snow White" is the heroine's change of environment. Her move from her parents' house to the companions' house provides the structural coda of the story. Like musical annotation, it signals a repetition of the primary melody or theme of the piece. Both in terms of narrative treatment of the transition between cycles (the dramatic transportation, hiatus, and subsequent renewal of action somewhere near the middle of the story) and in terms of the parallel pattern of action in both cycles (the coincidence in the action of the episodes in the first and second parts of the story), the structural repetition of the events in "Snow White" seems an explicit and significant feature of this narrative.

Some unusual treatments of "Snow White" also confirm the validity of the persecution pattern as an important part of that folktale's formal construction. For example, some versions of this tale include a third instance of this cycle of threat, hostility, and escape. In about 20 percent of the versions I have examined, a third repetition of hostilities follows the heroine's marriage. In these, the punishment that normally occurs at the conclusion of "Snow White" is omitted, and the heroine simply marries after her resuscitation. When the persecutor hears that the heroine has revived and married, the persecutor again tries to dispatch her rival. Thus, these longer versions, by incorporating a third cycle of persecution, further support the idea that these cycles of persecution are units of dramatic structure apparent to narrators, who may double or treble them in the story. . . .

STRUCTURE ENHANCES DRAMA, STYLE, AND THEME

The generic persecution pattern in "Snow White" serves a number of important purposes. First, it enhances the dramatic tension of the narrative. The events of the second part of the tale metaphorically duplicate the first part in new, expanded, and intensified context. By establishing a parallel structure of events, the narrator increases audience participation and concern by encouraging them to anticipate the perils of the heroine. The structural equivalence or correspondence of the events of the second part of "Snow White" to the events of the first generates echoes and reverberations of association and meaning, serving as warning and stimulation to the audience.

Second, the dramatic repetition serves a stylistic purpose; it divides the story roughly in half, provides a sense of balance and symmetry, and operates as an effective fundamental plot outline giving coherence and order to the story and organizing the details simply and sharply. The symmetry of the formal arrangement of the action, in which the persecutor in two separate situations or places threatens the heroine, confirms the folktale community's preference for order, balance, and consistency.

Finally, not only is the structural repetition in "Snow White" stylistically and dramatically a crucial element of the narrative but it also underscores that tale's thematic message. In essence, the structural pattern of episodes in "Snow White" recapitulates the personal development of the heroine; in other words, the sequence of episodes is structured to correspond to the basic trials and transitions of the maturing young woman in order to illustrate for the audience the process of maturation. This connection between theme and structure is evidenced by the way that the successive acts of the persecution pattern coincide with what may be considered three of the most crucial transitions in the heroine's life—puberty, marriage, and childbirth.

STRUCTURE DRAMATIZES GROWTH AND MATURITY

The first incidence of the persecution pattern appears, for a number of reasons, to correspond to the heroine's approaching sexual puberty. Generally, the heroine is at the appropriate age; even though some texts, like the Grimms', indicate the heroine is around seven, most portray her as being in her early teens and approaching young womanhood. Furthermore, the physiologically appropriate act of menstruation is suggested indirectly by the flow of blood that accompanies, in many versions, the first act of persecution.

Table 1: Pattern of Action in Three Versions of "Snow White"

GENERIC PATTERN (FUNCTIONS)	TYPOLOGICAL PATTERN (EPISODES)	VERSIONS* (MOTIFS)
Part 1		
Threat—the protagonist is threatened	Jealousy—persecutor becomes jealous of the heroine	(a) The persecutor learns from a magic mirror that the heroine is more beautiful
		(b) Stepmother resents her new stepdaughter
		(c) A stepmother feels that the father prefers the stepdaughter—breaks plates and glasses
Hostility—a hostile action is directed against the protagonist	Expulsion—the persecutor orders the heroine's death or otherwise expels her from home	(a) The queen orders a servant to kill the heroine; she is abandoned in the forest
		(b) Stepmother orders the heroine to water a dangerously situated basil plant
		(c) The father, on the request of the stepmother, abandons the heroine with a basket of food on a faraway mountain
Escape—the protagonist escapes from her predicament	Adoption—the heroine is rescued from her homeless plight and adopted by someone else	(a) The heroine is taken in by some dwarfs after they discover her in their house
		(b) An eagle carries the heroine to a fairy palace
		(c) The heroine secretly cooks and cleans at the palace of forty giants, who adopt her when they finally find her
Part 2		
Threat	Renewed Jealousy—the persecutor is informed that the heroine is still alive	(a) The persecutor learns from her magic mirror of the heroine's new home

Finally, the puberty period is suggested also by the heightened rivalries and tensions with the mother. This aspect of the physiological and sexual development of the heroine is illustrated by the motifs in which the suitors prefer the daughter to the mother or the magic mirror says that the heroine is more beautiful than the mother. These pubescent

GENERIC PATTERN (FUNCTIONS)	TYPOLOGICAL PATTERN (EPISODES)	VERSIONS* (MOTIFS)
	and still more beautiful	(b) The eagle boasts to the stepmother of the heroine's new home
		(c) The stepmother asks the sun if there is any prettier woman in the world and learns about the heroine's new home
Hostility	Death—the heroine dies at the hands of the persecutor or her agent	(a) The queen tries to kill the heroine with a staylace and a comb, and then succeeds with a poisoned apple
		(b) the stepmother asks a witch to kill the hero-ine, who tries first with poisoned sweetmeats, and finally succeeds with a poisoned dress
		(c) The stepmother tries to kill the heroine with a gold ring and then succeeds with a poisoned raisin
Escape	Resuscitation—the heroine is resuscitated, usually after someone sees and acquires her corpse	(a) A prince obtains the heroine's body; the coffin is jostled, and the heroine revives and marries the prince
		(b) A prince obtains the heroine's body; his mother removes the dress to clean it, and the heroine revives and marries the prince
		(c) A prince finds the heroine's body; his father presses the the heroine's chest and she spits up the raisin, revives and marries the prince

*The Typological Pattern decribes the major events of the fairy tale as repeated actions or episodes found in several variants.
(a) German version, (b) Italian version, (c) Asia Minor version

tensions are further illustrated by the motifs where the mother or stepmother tries to lock the heroine up in a room or cave or attempts to cut off her hair or otherwise disfigure her. Thus, the first act of the folktale appears to be set in a crucial period in the heroine's life when she is initially maturing into a young woman, and it metaphorically mirrors the anxieties and concerns typical of this adolescent stage of development.

The next act of the persecution pattern culminates in the heroine's marriage, illustrating the transition from adolescence to adulthood. The instance of the persecution pattern dramatizes the heroine's acceptance of the responsibilities and prerogatives of adulthood, especially sexuality, as illustrated in the motifs of the poisoned apple, dress, or slipper. The clothes and shoes are means of enhancing her physical beauty and confirm her status as a mature woman. With these clothes, the heroine is assuming the suits and trappings of womanhood. The other common motifs of the heroine eating various kinds of poisoned fruit (apples, grapes, raisins, and so on) represent the heroine metaphorically experiencing a socially euphemized sexual initiation. Thus, the second act dramatizes the heroine's transformation into a mature, married woman.

The final presentation of the persecution pattern (found only in the more unusual extended versions of "Snow White," but commonly a part of many other tale types of the "Persecuted heroine" cycle) coincides with the heroine's becoming a mother. The anxiety of motherhood and childbirth are depicted in the descriptions of the wife being accused of eating her newborn children or of giving birth to monsters or animals. Thus, the folktale appears to dramatize in these three acts of the persecution pattern, three significant stages in the growth of the child into a woman.

PATTERN OF TALE AS GUIDE

Presumably the purpose of this patterning of the folktale to correspond to a woman's typical life crises is that it attempts to assist the heroine in her passage through these major life changes by providing her with psychological, sociological, and philosophical instruction along the way. By tracing and anticipating her journey, the folktale serves as a guide and model for the young woman. Specifically, the key accomplishment of each of the acts is the relocation of the heroine in a new situation. Thus, the pattern of the tale is designed to encourage change and growth. Furthermore, there is an underlying development logic to the relocations. The heroine moves from the childish environment of the parents' home, to the adolescent environment of her friend's home, to the young woman's environment of her husband's home, and finally to the mature woman's environment of her own home. Thus, there is a progression in the ensuing acts of the persecution pattern toward self-independence and self-assertion, an underlying goal of achieving autonomy.

It must be noted that few of the tale types in the "Persecuted heroine" cycle, including "Snow White," present the full incidence of the pattern; they usually present only a portion of the overall moves and thus do not afford us the opportunity to see in one tale the entire life cycle. However, we do not expect every novel or play to present the entire life story; similarly, different tale types in the "Persecuted heroine" cycle may alternately focus on different stages in the heroine's development. The important point is that, generically, they may all be viewed as part of a larger narrative outline that does sketch the main changes in the typical overall experience of women. Thus, viewing the tales of the "Persecuted heroine" cycle as a group, we see that one very important function of this generic pattern is to illustrate the psycho-social development of the heroine, an outline of the normal process of maturation, as she passes through different stages in her life.

STRUCTURE MIRRORS SOCIAL RITUALS

Another way that the generic structure of the folktale of "Snow White" mirrors the development of a young woman may be seen in its emulation of the pattern of certain socially enacted rituals as identified by Arnold van Gennep. Van Gennep studied a wide variety of rituals associated with changes in an individual's status (such as puberty rituals, marriage rituals, and so on), and he found that these rituals follow a definite pattern in their depiction of the crossing of these thresholds. They dramatize the participants as going through the steps of separation, liminality, and reincorporation as a means of facilitating their transitions from one social status to another. This pattern appears to underlie the various acts of the "Persecuted heroine" cycle as well. The acts effect the heroine's separation from one setting, depict her liminal condition in the wilderness, and then reincorporate her into a new social situation. In the first act, the heroine is expelled, wanders through the forest, and then is adopted by the companions. In the second act, the heroine is killed, her body is then placed in a liminal situation (for example, tossed into the ocean or hung from a tree), and finally, she is married and moves into a new house. Thus, the order of the specific steps within each act of the "Persecuted heroine" cycle essentially duplicates the pattern of social rituals.

Presumably, the goal of the acts also duplicates the goal of the ritual to facilitate the heroine's transition from one social position to another. The acts correspond to certain important transitions in a young woman's life that would themselves logically be the subject of such rituals. As noted previously, the first act contains certain associations with puberty (bleeding, physiological maturation, sexual competition with another figure, or attraction to a father figure), the second act with marriage, and the third act with childbirth. All of these transitions are crucial changes for the young woman— changing first from an asexual to a sexual individual, from an unattached and unmarried woman to a married one, and finally from a childless woman to a child-rearing mother. These acts apparently serve the function of assisting the heroine in coping with these changes by echoing the traditional formulas used by rituals to guide initiates through those transitions. . . .

SIGNIFICANCE OF FAIRY TALE STRUCTURE

The purpose of the folktale is to assist the child in understanding and coping with her personal development by presenting in dramatic form the ritualized methods for coping with social and personal changes. For example, the heroine's death in the companions' house might be regarded as corresponding to van Gennep's observation that frequently young initiates in the coming-of-age rituals are regarded as being dead for a period and then reborn. Thus, Snow White's death may be seen as an illustration of the transformation of social position (dying in an old form in order to be reborn in a new one), rather than as simple acquiescence to sexist, passive role models. Furthermore, the quasi-human nature of many of the heroine's companions in this liminal situation is appropriately explained, in this light, as evidence of their role as liminal mediaries, fictional shamans as it were. Thus, we can see how the structure of "Snow White" is designed from the ritualistic model to dramatize the problems and the process of a young woman's maturation. As part of "Persecuted heroine" cycle, this particular folktale depicts two of the important stages in the growth of the child into a woman in order to serve the function of assisting the heroine in coping with these changes, becoming, in effect, a literary dramatization of the rites of passage.

In sum, we find that the narrative structures in "Snow White" serve useful functions for the audience of that folktale and are accordingly important elements of that story. Studying these structures helps us to realize the deceptive complexity of folktales. Like crystals that have been formed by years of pressure, folktales have an intricate beauty that is simultaneously the product of their exceptional longevity as well as an explanation for it. Given their history of being continually recreated by individual narrators in different social settings, under changing political conditions, with varying psychological concerns, it is no wonder that, under these pressures, they have become like diamonds, precisely structured and elegantly arranged gems of human expression.

America's "Cinderella"

Jane Yolen

Jane Yolen writes fairy tales and children's fiction.
Some of the best examples of her work, noted for
beautiful language and strong philosophical content,
can be found in *Tales of Wonder* and *Dragonfield and
Other Stories*. In the following article Yolen shows
how mass market popularizations have radically
modified many of the most famous fairy tales like
"Cinderella," rendering them pale reflections of the
original oral tales. Once a forthright and shrewd
heroine of considerable fortitude, the Cinderella of
the Disney film is a passive, pitiful dreamer whose
fate is solely in the hands of the rescuing prince. The
true meaning of the fairy tale, which relates to the
universal human capacity to draw on inner strengths
and rise triumphant out of difficult circumstances,
has been lost.

It is part of the American creed, recited subvocally along
with the pledge of allegiance in each classroom, that even a
poor boy can grow up to become president. The unliberated
corollary is that even a poor girl can grow up and become
the president's wife. This rags-to-riches formula was im-
mortalized in American children's fiction by the Horatio Al-
ger stories of the 1860s and by the Pluck and Luck nickel
novels of the 1920s.

It is little wonder, then, that Cinderella should be a peren-
nial favorite in the American folktale pantheon.

Yet how ironic that this formula should be the terms on
which "Cinderella" is acceptable to most Americans. "Cinderella" is *not* a story of rags to riches, but rather riches re-
covered; *not* poor girl into princess but rather rich girl (or
princess) rescued from improper or wicked enslavement; *not*
suffering Griselda enduring but shrewd and practical girl
persevering and winning a share of the power. It is really a

Excerpted from "America's Cinderella," by Jane Yolen, *Children's Literature in Education*, 1977. Adapted from the essay, "Touch Magic," published in *Touch Magic*, by Jane
Yolen, August House, 2000. Reprinted with permission from Kluwer Academic Publishers and Curtis Brown, Ltd.

story that is about "the stripping away of the disguise that conceals the soul from the eyes of others. . . ."

We Americans have it wrong. "Rumpelstiltskin," in which a miller tells a whopping lie and his docile daughter acquiesces in it to become queen, would be more to the point.

But we have been initially seduced by the Perrault cindergirl, who was, after all, the transfigured folk creature of a French literary courtier. Perrault's "Cendrillon" demonstrated the well-bred seventeenth-century female traits of gentility, grace, and selflessness, even to the point of graciously forgiving her wicked stepsisters and finding them noble husbands.

The American "Cinderella" is partially Perrault's. The rest is a spun-sugar caricature of her hardier European and Oriental forbears, who made their own way in the world, tricking the stepsisters with double-talk, artfully disguising themselves, or figuring out a way to win the king's son. The final bit of icing on the American Cinderella was concocted by that master candy-maker, Walt Disney, in the 1950s. Since then, America's Cinderella has been a coy, helpless dreamer, a "nice" girl who awaits her rescue with patience and a song. This Cinderella of the mass market books finds her way into a majority of American homes while the classic heroines sit unread in old volumes on library shelves.

Poor Cinderella. She has been unjustly distorted by storytellers, misunderstood by educators, and wrongly accused by feminists. Even as late as 1975, in the well-received volume *Womenfolk and Fairy Tales,* [American author] Rosemary Minard writes that Cinderella "would still be scrubbing floors if it were not for her fairy godmother." And Ms. Minard includes her in a sweeping condemnation of folk heroines as "insipid beauties waiting passively for Prince Charming."

Like many dialecticians [people skilled in critical inquiry] Ms. Minard reads the fairy tales incorrectly. Believing—rightly—that the fairy tales, as all stories for children, acculturate young readers and listeners, she has nevertheless gotten her target wrong. Cinderella is not to blame. Not the real, the true Cinderella. Ms. Minard should focus her sights on the mass-market Cinderella. She does not recognize the old Ash-girl for the tough, resilient heroine. The wrong Cinderella has gone to the American ball.

HISTORY OF THE CINDERELLA TALE

The story of Cinderella has endured for over a thousand years, surfacing in a literary source first in ninth-century China. It has been found from the Orient to the interior of South America and over five hundred variants have been located by folklorists in Europe alone. This best-beloved tale has been brought to life over and over and no one can say for sure where the oral tradition began. The European story was included by Charles Perrault in his 1697 collection *Histoires ou Contes du temps passé* as "Cendrillon." But even before that, the Italian Straparola had a similar story in a collection. Since there had been twelve editions of the Straparola book printed in French before 1694, the chances are strong that Perrault had read the tale "*Peau d' Ane*" (Donkey Skin).

[Australian folklorist] Joseph Jacobs, the indefatigable Victorian collector, once said of a Cinderella story he printed that it was "an English version of an Italian adaption of a Spanish translation of a Latin version of a Hebrew translation of an Arabic translation of an Indian original."

Perhaps it was not a totally accurate statement of that particular variant, but Jacobs was making a point about the perils of folktale-telling: each teller brings to a tale something of his/her own cultural orientation. Thus in China, where the "lotus foot," or tiny foot was such a sign of a woman's worth that the custom of foot-binding developed, the Cinderella tale lays emphasis on an impossibly small slipper as a clue to the heroine's identity. In seventeenth-century France, Perrault's creation sighs along with her stepsisters over the magnificent "gold flowered mantua"[1] and the "diamond stomacher."[2] In the Walt Disney American version, both movie and book form, Cinderella shares with the little animals a quality of "lovableness," thus changing the intent of the tale and denying the heroine her birthright of shrewdness, inventiveness, and grace under pressure.

Notice, though, that many innovations—the Chinese slipper, the Perrault godmother with her midnight injunction and her ability to change pumpkin into coach—become incorporated in later versions. Even a slip of the English translator's tongue (*de vair*, fur, into *de verre*, glass) becomes immortal-

1. a loose gown or cloak worn by women in the 1600s
2. ornamental covering for stomach and chest worn by women under the lacing of the bodice

ized. Such cross fertilization of folklore is phenomenal. And the staying power, across countries and centuries, of some of these inventions is notable. Yet glass slipper and godmother and pumpkin coach are not the common incidents by which a "Cinderella" tale is recognized even though they have become basic ingredients in the American story. Rather, the common incidents recognized by folklorists are these: an ill-treated though rich and worthy heroine in Cinders-disguise; the aid of a magical gift or advice by a beast/bird/mother substitute; the dance/festival/church scene where the heroine comes in radiant display; recognition through a token. So "Cinderella" and her true sister tales, [English variant] "Cap o' Rushes" with its King Lear judgement and "Catskin" wherein the father unnaturally desires his daughter, are counted.

[Scottish scholar and author] Andrew Lang's judgement that "a naked shoeless race could not have invented Cinderella," then, proves false. Variants have been found among the fur-wearing folk of Alaska and the native tribes in South Africa where shoes were not commonly worn.

"Cinderella" speaks to all of us in whatever skin we inhabit: the child mistreated, a princess or highborn lady in disguise bearing her trials with patience and fortitude. She makes intelligent decisions for she knows that wishing solves nothing without the concomitant action. We have each of us been that child. It is the longing of any youngster sent supperless to bed or given less than a full share at Christmas. It is the adolescent dream.

To make Cinderella less than she is, then, is a heresy of the worst kind. It cheapens our most cherished dreams, and it makes a mockery of the true magic inside us all—the ability to change our own lives, the ability to control our own destinies.

CINDERELLA COMES TO AMERICA

Cinderella first came to America in the nursery tales the settlers remembered from their own homes and told their children. Versions of these tales can still be found. Folklorist Richard Chase, for example, discovered "Rush Cape," an exact parallel of "Cap o' Rushes" with an Appalachian dialect in Tennessee, Kentucky, and South Carolina among others.

But when the story reached print, developed, was made literary, things began to happen to the hardy Cinderella. She suffered a sea change, a sea change aggravated by social conditions.

In the 1870s, for example, in the prestigious magazine for children *St. Nicholas,* there are a number of retellings or adaptations of "Cinderella." The retellings which merely translate European variants contain the hardy heroine. But when a new version is presented, a helpless Cinderella is born. G.B. Bartlett's "Giant Picture-Book," which was considered "a curious novelty [that] can be produced . . . by children for the amusement of their friends . . ." presents a weepy, prostrate young blonde (the instructions here are quite specific) who must be "aroused from her sad revery" by a godmother. Yet in the truer Cinderella stories, the heroine is not this catatonic. For example, in the Grimm "Cinder-Maid," though she weeps, she continues to perform the proper rites and rituals at her mother's grave, instructing the birds who roost there to:

Make me a lady fair to see,
Dress me as splendid as can be.

And in "The Dirty Shepherdess," a "Cap o' Rushes" variant from France, ". . . she dried her eyes, and made a bundle of her jewels and her best dresses and hurriedly left the castle where she was born." In the *St. Nicholas* "Giant Picture-Book" she has none of this strength of purpose. Rather, she is manipulated by the godmother until the moment she stands before the prince where she speaks "meekly" and "with downcast eyes and extended hand."

St. Nicholas was not meant for the mass market. It had, in [American children's writer] Selma Lanes' words, "a patrician call to a highly literate readership." But nevertheless, Bartlett's play instructions indicate how even in the more literary reaches of children's books a change was taking place.

However, to truly mark this change in the American "Cinderella," one must turn specifically to the mass-market books, merchandised products that masquerade as literature but make as little lasting literary impression as a lollipop. They, after all, serve the majority the way the storytellers of the village used to serve. They find their way into millions of homes.

Mass market books are almost as old as colonial America. The chapbooks of the eighteenth and nineteenth century, crudely printed tiny paperbacks, were the source of most children's reading in the early days of our country. Originally these were books imported from Europe. But slowly

American publishing grew. In the latter part of the nineteenth century one firm stood out—McLoughlin Bros. They brought bright colors to the pages of children's books. In a series selling for twenty-five cents per book, *Aunt Kate's Series*, bowdlerized folk tales emerged. "Cinderella" was there, along with "Red Riding Hood," "Puss in Boots," and others. Endings were changed, innards cleaned up, and good triumphed with very loud huzzahs. Cinderella is the weepy, sentimentalized pretty girl incapable of helping herself. In contrast, one only has to look at the girl in "Cap o' Rushes" who comes to a great house and asks "Do you want a maid?" and when refused, goes on to say ". . . I ask no wages and do any sort of work." And she does. In the end, when the master's young son is dying of love for the mysterious lady, she uses her wits to work her way out of the kitchen. Even in Perrault's "Cinderilla," when the fairy godmother runs out of ideas for enchantment and "was at a loss for a coachman, I'll go and see, says Cinderilla, if there be never a rat in the rattrap, we'll make a coachman of him. You are in the right, said her godmother, go and see."

Hardy, helpful, inventive, that was the Cinderella of the old tales but not of the mass market in the nineteenth century. Today's mass-market books are worse. These are the books sold in supermarket and candystore, even lining the shelves of many of the best bookstores. There are pop-up Cinderellas, coloring-book Cinderellas, scratch-and-sniff Cinderellas, all inexpensive and available. The point in these books is not the story but the *gimmick*. These are books which must "interest 300,000 children, selling their initial print order in one season and continuing strong for at least two years after that." Compare that with the usual trade publishing house print order of a juvenile book—10,000 copies which an editor hopes to sell out in a lifetime of that title.

THE ORIGINAL CINDERELLA TALE

All the folk tales have been gutted. But none so changed, I believe, as "Cinderella." For the sake of Happy Ever After, the mass-market books have brought forward a good, malleable, forgiving little girl and put her in Cinderella's slippers. However, in most of the Cinderella tales there is no forgiveness in the heroine's heart. No mercy. Just justice. In "Rushen Coatie" and "The Cinder-Maid," [a European variant identified by Jacobs] the elder sisters hack off their toes and heels in order to fit the shoe. Cinderella never stops them, never implies that she has the matching slipper. In fact, her tattletale birds warn the prince in "Rushen Coatie":

Hacked Heels and Pinched Toes
Behind the young prince rides,
But Pretty Feet and Little Feet
Behind the cauldron bides.

Even more graphically, they call out in "Cinder-Maid"

Turn and peep, turn and peep,
There's blood within the shoe;
A bit is cut from off the heel
And a bit from off the toe.

Cinderella never says a word of comfort. And in the least bowdlerized of the German and Nordic tales, the two sisters come to the wedding "the elder was at the right side and the younger at the left, and the pigeons pecked out one eye from each of them. Afterwards, as they came back, the elder was on the left, and the younger at the right, and then the pigeons pecked out the other eye from each. And thus, for their wickedness and falsehood, they were punished with blindness all their days." That's a far cry from Perrault's heroine who "gave her sisters lodgings in the palace, and married them the same day to two great lords of the court." And further still from [American author] Nola Langner's Scholastic paperback "Cinderella."

[The sisters] began to cry.
    They begged Cinderella to forgive them for being so mean to her.
    Cinderella told them they were forgiven.
    "I am sure you will never be mean to me again," she said.
    "Oh, never," said the older sister.
    "Never, ever," said the younger sister.

Missing, too, from the mass-market books is the shrewd, even witty Cinderella. In a Wonder Book entitled "Bedtime Stories," a 1940s adaptation from Perrault, we find a Cinderella who talks to her stepsisters "in a shy little voice." Even Perrault's heroine bantered with her stepsisters, asking them leading questions about the ball while secretly and deliciously knowing the answers. In the Wonder Book, however, the true wonder is that Cinderella ever gets to be princess. Even face-to-face with the prince, she is unrecognized until she dons her magic ballgown. Only when her clothes are transformed does the prince know his true love.

WALT DISNEY'S CINDERELLA

In 1949, Walt Disney's film *Cinderella* burst onto the American scene. The story in the mass market has not been the same since.

The film came out of the studio at a particularly trying time for Disney. He had been deserted by the intellectuals who had been champions of this art for some years. Because of World War II, the public was more interested in war films than cartoons. But when *Cinderella,* lighter than light, was released it brought back to Disney—and his studio—all of his lost fame and fortune. The film was one of the most profitable of all time for the studio, grossing $4.247 million dollars in the first release alone. The success of the movie opened the floodgates of "Disney Cinderella" books.

Golden Press's *Walt Disney's Cinderella* set the new pattern for America's Cinderella. This book's text is coy and condescending. (Sample: "And her best friends of all were—guess who—the mice!") The illustrations are poor cartoons. And Cinderella herself is a disaster. She cowers as her sisters rip her homemade ball gown to shreds. (Not even homemade by Cinderella, but by the mice and birds.) She answers her stepmother with whines and pleadings. She is a sorry excuse for a heroine, pitiable and useless. She cannot perform even a simple action to save herself, though she is warned by her friends, the mice. She does not hear them because she is "off in a world of dreams." Cinderella begs, she whimpers, and at last has to be rescued by—guess who—the mice!

There is also an easy-reading version published by Random House, *Walt Disney's Cinderella.* This Cinderella commits the further heresy of cursing her luck. "How I did wish to go to the ball," she says. "But it is no use. Wishes never come true."

But in the fairy tales wishes have a habit of happening—*wishes accompanied by the proper action,* bad wishes as well as good. That is the beauty of the old stories and their wisdom as well.

Take away the proper course of action, take away Cinderella's ability to think for herself and act for herself, and you are left with a tale of wishes-come-true-regardless. But that is not the way of the fairy tale. As [Australian-born folklorist and children's book writer] P.L. Travers so wisely puts it, "If that were so, wouldn't we all be married to princes?"

The mass-market American "Cinderellas" have presented the majority of American children with the wrong dream. They offer the passive princess, the "insipid beauty waiting . . . for Prince Charming" that Rosemary Minard objects to, and thus acculturate millions of girls and boys. But it is the wrong Cinderella and the magic of the old tales has been falsified, the true meaning lost, perhaps forever.

CHAPTER 4

Influence on Literature

Fairy
Tales

Charles Dickens and the Fairy Tale as Social Commentary

Michael Kotzin

In *Dickens and the Fairy Tale*, Michael Kotzin, from Tel-Aviv University, examines the pervasive influence of fairy tales on the life and work of Charles Dickens. Transposing the genre to an urban setting and giving the nursery tales of his childhood a "higher form" were among Dickens' intentions. His way of perceiving the world could be best expressed in fairy tale terms, and making allegorical and satirical use of the genre aided Dickens' serious social commentary. In the following extract, Kotzin says that Dickens drew upon fairy tale motifs, narrative patterns, and fairy tale-type characters and settings to help people sense romance in the everyday world and grasp the need for moral improvement. His popularity then and now owes some legacy to the magic and mystery of the traditional fairy tale.

As entertainer and social critic, artist and tormented man, Dickens was never far from the fairy tale. When he was a child, it showed him an imaginary world which was both fun and horrifying; as he grew up, he discovered the real world to indeed be that way. Part of the horror was of man's making—the result of social conditions which, it seemed, could be corrected, and Dickens called upon the entertaining medium of the fairy tale in an attempt to bring about change. Another part of it was not of man's making, though— was, it seemed, the permanent nature of things; all man could do was perceive his situation and perhaps wish himself free of it, and that too could be done by reference to the fairy tale.

Excerpted from *Dickens and the Fairy Tale,* by Michael Kotzin. Reprinted with permission from Bowling Green Popular Press.

The joy which fairy tales brought the child Charles Dickens is indicated in articles he later wrote. In "A Christmas Tree" he remembers Little Red Riding-Hood as "my first love. I felt that if I could have married Little Red Riding-Hood, I should have known perfect bliss." The horror is also indicated. In "Nurse's Stories," he talks about the "dark corners" of the mind which he says nurses are "responsible for" and which "we are forced to go back to, against our wills," and he suggests how terrified he had been when he had heard his nurse's stories.

I do not believe that these stories formed Dickens' imagination; but they fed it in important ways. Dickens seems to have had a natural taste for both the imaginative fun and the frightening terror of the works. Unlike David Copperfield, he did not have to turn to such tales to protect himself from a Murdstone, to keep alive his "fancy, and [his] hope of something beyond that place and time", and yet he did turn to them, and like David, did imagine himself in them. And after being free of his nurse, he did not have to continue to subject himself to tales of terror, and yet he also did that. He seems to have reacted to the stories much as did [Romantic poet Samuel Taylor] Coleridge, who remembered reading his father's copy of the *Arabian Nights* "over and over again before my fifth birthday," who reflected how he had looked at the book with "a strange mixture of obscure dread and intense desire" and then read it in the sunlight. When Dickens left the childhood world of books, his experiences confirmed what, partly because of fairy tales, he already knew about life. And the fairy tales then provided him with a vocabulary of references, images, and motifs with which he could express his vision of the world to others.

[English novelist] George Gissing, in making a similar point, said:

> Oddly enough, Dickens seems to make more allusions throughout his work to the *Arabian Nights* than to any other book or author. He is not given to quoting, or making literary references; but those fairy tales of the East supply him with a good number of illustrations, and not only in his early novels. Is it merely fanciful to see in this interest, not of course an explanation, but a circumstance illustrative, of that habit of mind which led him to discover infinite romance in the obscurer life of London? Where the ordinary man sees nothing but everyday habit, Dickens is filled with the perception of marvellous possibilities. Again and again he has put the spirit

of the *Arabian Nights* into his pictures of life by the river Thames. . . . He sought for wonders amid the dreary life of common streets; and perhaps in this direction also his intellect was encouraged when he made acquaintance with the dazzling Eastern fables, and took them alternately with that more solid nutriment of the eighteenth-century novel.

PERCEIVING THE WORLD IN FAIRY TALE TERMS

His desire to somehow reproduce the fairy tales he read began when Dickens was a child. One of his earliest writings was a play called *Misnar,* the Sultan of India, a work which Forster says was "founded (and very literally founded, no doubt) on one of the *Tales of the Genii.*" Later, modifying the tales, he was like David Copperfield, who says that when he was in London working at Murdstone and Grinby's he "fitted my old books to my altered life, and made stories for myself, out of the streets, and out of men and women." Throughout his career as a writer he probably occasionally found himself in the position of Steerforth, who says: "At odd dull times, nursery tales come up into the memory, unrecognized for what they are." Fairy tales, used consciously and unconsciously, served Dickens well in his attempt to render his perception of the world and man's experience in it.

One of the things he saw was that the world was fantastic, enchanting. This he could describe by references to fairy tales. In a letter to Forster from America he described Cincinnati as having "risen out of the forest like an Arabian-night city." Later from Venice he wrote him: "The wildest visions of the Arabian Nights are nothing to the piazza of Saint Mark, and the first impression of the inside of the church." And still later he wrote Lever: "Paris is more amazing than ever, and the Genius of the Lamp is always building Palaces in the night." What is often called his child's view of the universe, his manner of portraying the world in much the same way as it is portrayed in fairy tales, seems truly to have derived from his natural way of perceiving things, and is expressed in letters, articles, and novels alike.

Another thing he saw in the world was that it needed correction. This too he talked about in fairy-tale terms. In a speech to the Polytechnic Institution in Birmingham on February 28, 1844, he developed the *Arabian Nights* story of the sealed casket as an allegory on the locked up Spirit of Ignorance in the modern age which, if released in time, "will bless, restore, and reanimate society," and if not will destroy it. He enlarged upon the device of allegory in articles in [the periodical he published] *Household Words* in which he took advantage of the fun of fairy tales while using them to serious purpose.

FAIRY TALES USED FOR SERIOUS SOCIAL COMMENT

Elaborating on one aspect of contemporary pantomimes, which frequently included topical satire, he used the "low" form of the fairy tale to burlesque "high" modern events. In "Frauds on the Fairies," after directly attacking Cruikshank's propagandistic adaptations of fairy tales, he himself rewrote "Cinderella," making fun of Cruikshank but at the same time, by showing how the story would appear if written "according to Total-abstinence, Peace Society, and Bloomer principles, and expressly for their propagation," burlesquing the people who follow and advocate those principles. In "Prince Bull. A Fairy Tale," Dickens used the fairy-tale format for an entire article. Bull, of course, is England. He is cursed with "a tyrannical old godmother whose name was Tape. She was a Fairy, this Tape, and was a bright red all over. She was disgustingly prim and formal, and could never bend herself a hair's breadth this way or that way, out of her naturally crooked shape." This Fairy, by saying "Tape," can upset anything, and that is what she does when Bull goes to war with "Prince Bear"(Russia), and when Bull tries to get new servants (a new government) to correct matters. Thus, Dickens used the seemingly frivolous form of the fairy tale to burlesque bitterly the harmful effects of the tyrannical red tape damaging England during the Crimean War period. . . .

The novels also use fairy tales for satirical purposes. A cruel police magistrate [in *Oliver Twist*] is called one of the "presiding Genii." An inflated person like Pecksniff [in *Martin Chuzzlewit*] is called a moral man. . . . It was once said of him by a homely admirer, that he had a Fortunatus's purse of good sentiments in his inside. In this particular he was like the girl in the fairy tale, except that if they were not actual diamonds which fell from his lips, they were the very brightest paste, and shone prodigiously.

A utilitarian teacher [in *Hard Times*] is called "a dry Ogre. . . . I only use the word to express a monster in a lecturing castle, with Heaven knows how many heads manipulated into one, taking childhood captive and dragging it into gloomy statistical dens by the hair." The nouveau-riche Veneerings [in *Our Mutual Friend*] "have a house out of the Tales of the Genii, and give dinners out of the Arabian Nights." The ghastly Lady Tippins, called a "fragile nursling of the fairies," flirts with Eugene and "playfully insinuates that she (a self-evident proposition) is Beauty, and he Beast." By making such allusions the author can seem good-natured even when he is calling a man a "monster," and he can ironically show that Victorian England, the worse for it, is not the world of fairy tales.

DICKENS' MORAL PURPOSE

Fairy tales are appropriate for Dickensian satire: they traditionally take the side of the underdog against authority. And the Victorian view of them made them appropriate for other Dickensian purposes as well, in speeches, articles, and fiction. The same kind of valuable imaginative entertainment that Dickens thought fairy tales themselves could provide he thought could be provided by novels which used fairy tales. Like fairy tales, such novels could provide the moral improvement which comes when a man's heart is touched. What fairy tales do for children and adults, fiction using fairy tales can also do, for more sophisticated adults. Such fiction can have the kind of effect that the fairy tales heard by Sissy Jupe's father [in *Hard Times*] had on him.

> "And he liked them?" said Louisa. . . .
> "O very much! They kept him, many times, from what did him real harm. And often and often of a night, he used to forget all his troubles in wondering whether the Sultan would let the lady go on with the story, or would have her head cut off before it was finished."
> "And your father was always kind? To the last?" asked Louisa. . . .
> "Always, always!" returned Sissy, clasping her hands. "Kinder and kinder than I can tell."

The fullest, most explicit elaboration of Dickens' purposes in using fairy tales in his fiction was given by [historian and biographer John] Forster, who, in discussing the Christmas Books, said:

> No one was more intensely fond than Dickens of old nursery tales, and he had a secret delight in feeling that he was here only giving them a higher form. The social and manly virtues he desired to teach, were to him not less the charm of the

ghost, the goblin, and the fairy fancies of his childhood; however rudely set forth in those earlier days. What now were to be conquered were the more formidable dragons and giants that had their places at our own hearths, and the weapons to be used were of a finer quality than the 'ice-brook's temper.' With brave and strong restraints, what is evil in ourselves was to be subdued; with warm and gentle sympathies, what is bad or unreclaimed in others was to be redeemed; the Beauty was to embrace the Beast, as in the divinest of all those fables; the star was to rise out of the ashes, as in our much-loved Cinderella; and we were to play the Valentine with our wilder brothers, and bring them back with brotherly care to civilization and happiness.

Dickens himself seldom preached his lesson. As journalist and novelist, he wrote to amuse his readers and to do what he wanted done: to stimulate their imaginations. He wrote as an entertainer whose sources were in a popular folk tradition which included the fairy tale. As a serial novelist sensitive to his audience and later as a reciter of his fiction he was a modern popular story teller. He often alluded in fun to the fairy tales he drew upon. Like many other adult adaptors of fairy-tale material, including Perrault and Hoffmann, he mocked the childish stories and often referred to them with tongue in cheek. But like them too, he seems to have done so in order to also be able to use them seriously. And Dickens was serious. He entertained his fellow men not only to gratify himself but also in order to save them, individually and collectively. He wrote a series of novels which give the old nursery tales "a higher form," which not only, like some of his articles, frequently allude to fairy tales and follow their narrative patterns, but which place fairy-tale type characters in fairy-tale type worlds, and partly create the effects of fairy tales. In so doing he led the way in providing the Victorian novel with a source of the fantastic which is more appropriate to it than the Gothic novel, more normal and more domestic, but which still adds mystery and magic, and which evokes universal joys and fears and the timeless world of dream.

Modern Anti–Fairy Tale Poetry

Wolfgang Mieder

In *Disenchantments: An Anthology of Modern Fairy Tale Poetry,* Wolfgang Mieder, eminent folklorist from the University of Vermont, explains that fairy tales have inspired literary variations in the form of plays, operas, stories, and, particularly, ballads and poems. Modern fairy tale poetry, a subgenre of lyric poetry, draws on the fairy tale motifs and well-known plots to make serious commentary on modern day life. Like the original oral fairy tales, this poetry is principally for adults to help them deal with hardships in everyday life. While on the surface the satire and cynicism prevalent in the poetry is far from the optimism of the traditional tales, the poems are designed to shock the reader into new awareness. They are powerful vehicles advocating social change and personal transformation.

Interest in fairy tales has increased tremendously in the last ... decades [of the twentieth century]. Beautifully illustrated editions of Grimms' tales in particular can be found in bookstores everywhere, and children's ongoing fascination with fairy tales is matched by the serious attention that scholars pay to them. Cultural and literary historians, sociologists, folklorists, psychologists, and others who have studied the deeper meanings of fairy tales all attest to the universality of these traditional narratives. Although they depict a supernatural world with its miraculous, magical, and numinous aspects, fairy tales present in a symbolic fashion common problems and concerns of humanity. They deal with all aspects of social life and human behavior: not only such rites of passage as birth, courtship, betrothal, marriage, old age, and death, but also episodes that are typical in most people's

Excerpted from *Disenchantments: An Anthology of Modern Fairy Tale Poetry* (University Press of New England: Hanover, 1985) by Wolfgang Mieder. Reprinted with permission from the author.

lives. The emotional range includes in part love, hate, distrust, joy, persecution, happiness, murder, rivalry, and friendship, and often the same tale deals with such phenomena in contrasting pairs, that is, good versus evil, success versus failure, benevolence versus malevolence, poverty versus wealth, fortune versus misfortune, victory versus defeat, compassion versus harshness, modesty versus indecency; in short, black versus white. What distinguishes all fairy tales from other oral or written narratives is, of course, that the conflicts are resolved in the end. Happiness, joy, contentment, and harmony become the optimistic expression of a world as it should be, where all good wishes are fulfilled.

Little wonder that such tales of a poeticized and perfect world have seemed appropriate literature for young and innocent children since the Victorian age. A child learns from them that certain problems, dangers, and ordeals may, if met with perseverance, be surmounted. Since fairy tales usually present a simple plot that proceeds from a negative state to a positive resolution, child psychologists have long argued that children will understand their symbolism to mean that transformations are necessary, that changes will and must take place, and that everything will work out in the end. Children will reinterpret their own lives and experiences according to the fairy tale messages, even though this process might go on subconsciously, and they will gain an optimistic and future-oriented world view of their own. They will learn to solve their conflicts imaginatively; ultimately, they will become independent and socially responsible people, and will reach a higher realm of being where the search for personal pleasure is replaced by a sound understanding of social reality. But these are utopian hopes and dreams of psychologists, for obviously fairy tales alone do not make a perfect human being. They can, however, help children as well as adults to understand universal human problems better, for at the level of a children's story or of adult literature, fairy tales provide a key to a better understanding of one's own being and the world at large.

FAIRY TALES WERE ADULT FARE

There can be no doubt that traditional fairy tales are still told, read, heard on the radio, or seen on the television or movie screen, and that children continue to be enchanted by them. While for children they are absorbing and wonderful fantasies, it must not be forgotten that these narratives stem from earlier times and that they contain elements of social history for a time far removed from the present. Their morality and ethics do not necessarily correspond to the modern value system of a technological society. They often camouflaged the trials of oppressed people against unfair rulers, the conflict between the have-nots and the haves, the desires for a fairer political and social order, and so on. Behind the poetic symbolism of many fairy tales lies the gruesome reality of the Middle Ages from which the common folk escaped into the stories that we now know as fairy tales. In other words, the tales that have been read as beautiful and simple stories of luck, happiness and wish fulfillment by generations of children were in fact not invented for children. Only with the Brothers Grimm did these adult stories become the *Children- and Household Tales (Kinder- und Hausmärchen)* that have influenced youth ever since. But the "sweet" and "cute" tales conceal the frustrations of adults of another age who longed for a better and fairer world, where good would win out over evil, and where in fact all people could live happily ever after.

PREVAILING MOOD OF CYNICISM

It must not come as a surprise, therefore, that when rereading or remembering the fairy tales with which they became so well acquainted as children, adults often respond quite differently from the way psychologists predict. Once adults have lost their naive understanding of the fairy tale world, they tend to read fairy tales critically rather than symbolically. Having relinquished their dreams of a perfect world of happiness, love, and optimism, they question the positive value system of the fairy tales. Adults do not accept the positive solution of the old fairy tale any longer but, rather, are occupied with real-life problems. If unhappy and oppressed adults of earlier times formulated these tales as an escape from an ugly reality, modern people, who have often accepted a pessimistic world view at the expense of the optimistic view expressed in fairy tales, identify with the problems of former times that are also their own.

Thus it is of no consequence that Snow White, for example, finds her prince at the end and lives happily ever after. Much more interesting and "real" is her relationship with her stepmother (or evil mother), that is, the timeless mother-daughter conflict, or the sexual implications of her staying alone at the house with seven dwarfs who quickly, in modern interpretations, become transfigured into perverts.

It is the individual problems of the fairy tales that modern adults concentrate on, since these reflect today's social reality. After all, what normally intelligent person would possibly admit to believing in the optimism of the fairy tales? A good dose of negativism is inherent in our world view and probably rightfully. Although inside we may wish for a better existence, we are often preoccupied with problems that prevent us from finding that happy end. The positive vision of the fairy tales seems to become lost in a world riddled by pessimism, skepticism, and cynicism.

INTERPLAY OF TRADITION AND INNOVATION

Yet modern mankind cannot and probably should not free itself from the traditional fairy tales. Luckily they are common knowledge, and as such are familiar to almost everybody, as only the Bible and a few other great written works are. Because they are part of our heritage, we can communicate with them and through them. Fairy tales are not only stories of enchantment for children but also a form of entertainment (humorous and serious) for adults who reinterpret them innovatively. Since modern interpreters of the tales often look critically at particular problems in individual fairy tales, the tales are seen as reflections of a troubled society, as a critical view of the belief in perfect love, as a concern with sexual matters and so on. The happy end of the old fairy tale is more often than not forgotten or negated. Such modern reinterpretations of fairy tales are most effective when contrasted with the traditional version, that is, when wishful thinking and reality are juxtaposed. The resulting interplay of tradition and innovation not only takes place in people's personal reactions to fairy tales but can also be seen in movies and on television, on records, in advertisements, in comic strips, and in cartoons. The popularity of fairy tales or at least individual fairy tale motifs in the mass media is increasing and speaks of the regeneration of fairy tales.

ANTI-FAIRY TALE POETRY

A questioning reaction to fairy tales became common in the middle of the nineteenth century. Such well-known classics as "Sleeping Beauty," "Little Red Riding Hood," and "Snow White" among others inspired poetic variations in the form of plays, operas, stories, and, above all, ballads and poems. At the beginning of this vogue these adaptations, especially those cast into lyrical forms, were usually more or less precise retellings of the tale. Such authors as Tom Hood, John Greenleaf Whittier, James N. Barker, Frances Sargent Osgood, Bret Harte, Samuel Rogers, and even Alfred Tennyson delighted in writing such poems. But by the turn of the century a tendency to confront the fairy tale world—through humor, irony, or satire—with a less favorable reality became discernible. Questions of guilt, deception, marriage, love, emancipation, and so on, began to be raised, changing some of these earlier fairy tale poems to anti-fairy tales.

CHARACTERISTICS OF MODERN FAIRY TALE POETRY

Realistic reinterpretations of entire fairy tales or certain motifs have become the rule in modern fairy tale poetry, a subgenre of lyric poetry that has received little recognition from the scholarly world. Even though some literary historians have commented on the fairy tale poems by such poets as Randall Jarrell and Anne Sexton, the fact that many modern poets have written fascinating poems either based on fairy tales or at least alluding to them has been overlooked. At the beginning of this century James Whitcomb Riley composed a number of generally traditional fairy tale poems, and his "Maymie's Story of Red Riding Hood" was even written in dialect. But contrast such a poem with the recent retelling of several popular fairy tales for children and adults by Roald Dahl. In his lengthy poems the fairy tales are restated in the jargon of the modern world, so that one finds in his poems, for example, such words as "discos," "pistols," and "panty hose." Dahl has brought fairy tales up to date, somewhat as James Thurber did in his short prose texts.

A few poems still exist that contain somewhat positive reactions to the perfect world of the fairy tale endings. As an example, Joy Davidman's "Rapunzel" poem, "The Princess in the Ivory Tower," comes to mind; though even in this poem it is not clear whether the prince will reach his beloved or not. And the poem "Reading the Brothers Grimm to Jenny" by Lisel Mueller, clearly written by a mother for a child, also does not remain unproblematic, juxtaposing as it does the wonderful world of fairy tales and the dangerous

world of reality. Only a few poems retain the peace and harmony reached in the conclusions of the original tales. Yet,
with the exception of some humorous poems that are in fact
ridiculous nonsense verses, the modern Anglo-American
fairy tale poems are critical reactions to fairy tales that are
no longer believed or accepted. Transformed into parodistic,
satirical, or cynical anti-fairy tales, these poems often contain serious social criticisms. By reading these modern ren-
derings the reader is supposed to reevaluate societal problems. The unexpressed hope is perhaps that such alienating
anti-fairy tales might eventually be transformed again to
real fairy tales in a better world. Many fairy tale poems are
therefore deeply felt moral statements.

POETRY ADVOCATES CHANGE

Modern fairy tale poems concern themselves with every
imaginable human problem: there are poems about love and
hate, war and politics, marriage and divorce, responsibility
and criminality, and, of course, emancipation as well as sexual politics. Such productive fairy tale poets as Sara Hender-
son Hay, Anne Sexton, and Olga Broumas deal specifically
with women's concerns and do not shy away from homosex-
ual issues. Their poems are never vulgar or promiscuous—
they are sincere personal expressions. The emotional inten-
sity of these poems can perhaps best be expressed in the
lyrical form and by means of fairy tale elements. Psychological investigations of fairy tales have shown that they can be
interpreted sexually, and it is therefore not surprising to see
modern renditions along these lines. But sex is only one major theme of these poems. Many of them also deal with such
problems as greed, cruelty, deception, lovelessness, vanity,
materialism, power, and irresponsibility. The adult world is
simply not perfect any more. The philosophical fairy tale poems by Randall Jarrell especially capture the frustrations
that modern mankind experiences in a world void of happy
endings. But as was stated previously, many of the pessimistic statements conceal a quiet hope for a better world
where these anti-fairy tales will once again become fairy
tales. As Jarrell puts it at the end of his poem "The Märchen
(Grimm's Tales)":

> It was not power that you lacked, but wishes.
> Had you not learned—have we not learned, from tales

Neither of beasts nor kingdoms nor their Lord,
But of our own hearts, the realm of death—
Neither to rule nor die? to change, to change!

Changes are necessary in an increasingly complex world. Let us hope that such transformations lead humanity to positive solutions to its difficult problems.

Contemporary Feminist Fairy Tales

Sheldon Cashdan

Contemporary feminist writers of fairy tales give new twists to the classical tales and jolt the reader into questioning assumptions about sexual stereotypes and traditional happy endings. In the following extract, Sheldon Cashdan analyzes tales written by James Thurber, Jane Yolen, Jeanne Desy, and Judith Viorst which portray a new type of heroine—bold, resourceful and looking to satisfy her own desires rather than being the object of someone else's. Sheldon Cashdan is an Emeritus Professor of Psychology at the University of Massachusetts.

One afternoon a big wolf waited in a dark forest for a little girl to come along carrying a basket of food to her grandmother. Finally, a little girl did come along and she was carrying a basket of food. "Are you carrying that basket to your grandmother?" asked the wolf. The little girl said yes, she was. So the wolf asked her where her grandmother lived and the little girl told him and he disappeared into the wood.

When the little girl opened the door of her grandmother's house she saw that there was somebody in bed with a nightcap and nightgown on. She had approached no nearer than twenty-five feet from the bed when she saw that it was not her grandmother but the wolf, for even in a nightcap a wolf does not look any more like your grandmother than the Metro-Goldwyn lion looks like Calvin Coolidge. So the little girl took an automatic out of her basket and shot the wolf dead.

Moral: It is not so easy to fool little girls nowadays as it used to be.

James Thurber's *The Little Girl and the Wolf* presents us with a much different vision of Little Red Riding Hood than we are accustomed to. The image of the little girl in the red cape defending herself—with a forty-five automatic, no less—is a

Excerpted from *The Witch Must Die: How Fairy Tales Shape Our Lives*, by Sheldon Cashdan. Copyright © 1999 by Sheldon Cashdan. Reprinted with permission from Basic Books, a member of Perseus Books, L.L.C.

far cry from the traditional picture of Red Riding Hood found in children's storybooks.

NEW FAIRY TALE HEROINES

As we enter the twenty-first century, our notions of fairy tales and the meaning they have for children are likely to undergo change. But that is to be expected. Fairy tales have always been products of the culture and era of which they are a part. It thus is not surprising that an entire genre of feminist tales has appeared in recent years that seeks to challenge many of the underlying fairy-tale assumptions about male-female relationships. Rather than giving us heroines who are passive, submissive, and self-sacrificing, tales with a feminist bent feature a heroine who is bold, resourceful, and sassy. She is more likely to rescue the prince than the other way around. Indeed, in some contemporary fairy tales, there isn't even a prince.

Jane Yolen's Cinderella-like tale *The Moon Ribbon* is a case in point. In it, the widowed father of a girl named Sylva decides to remarry after many years without a wife. Much to Sylva's consternation, the woman he marries is selfish and mean-spirited, as are her two daughters from a previous marriage. Soon after arriving, the new wife dismisses the servants and saddles Sylva with all the household chores, forcing her to clean, cook, and toil in the fields.

One day, when Sylva is cleaning out an old desk, she comes across a silver-tinted ribbon that had belonged to her mother. The ribbon is the color of her mother's hair, and Sylva cherishes it as a reminder of her mother and their time together. Her stepsisters are attracted to the pretty ribbon and try to take it from Sylva, but she manages to safeguard it. It is the only concrete reminder she has of happier days.

One night while Sylva is lamenting her circumstances, the ribbon magically turns into a river and transports her to a distant kingdom. There she meets a silver-haired woman living in a great house at the edge of a forest. The woman identifies herself as Sylva's mother and, in an emotional exchange, exhorts Sylva to reach deep within herself for strength and inspiration. The young girl returns home with a memento of her visit, a precious crystal.

When Sylva tells her stepmother about her adventure, she scoffs at the girl's story. Though she cannot explain how Sylva has come into possession of the gemstone, she confiscates it, sells it, and keeps the proceeds for herself. Through the magic of the ribbon, Sylva returns a second time to the mysterious house by the forest, where she again encounters her spiritual benefactor. This time her mother presents her with two fiery-red jewels. Sylva returns home, where she is again confronted by her stepmother and ordered to turn over the stones. Sylva refuses.

"I *cannot*," she tells her stepmother.

"Girl, give it here," the stepmother insists, a menacing look in her eyes.

This time Sylva responds, "I *will* not."

HEROINES STAND ON OWN TWO FEET

The change from "I *can* not" to "I *will* not" signifies Sylva's transformation from a passive, subservient child to an active, self-assertive young woman. Her transformation, significantly, takes place without the help of a prince but rather from her experiences with a nurturant adult female. In Yolen's tale, there is no fancy ball, no magic slipper, and no male presence to save Sylva from a malevolent stepmother. Left to her own devices, the heroine asserts her independence and carves out a new identity for herself.

As in most stories that owe allegiance to *Cinderella*, the stepmother and her daughters in *The Moon Ribbon* are punished for their evil ways. The stepmother, believing that the ribbon will point the way to great riches, takes the ribbon from Sylva in lieu of the jewels and heads across a meadow, triumphantly waving the ribbon over her head. Halfway across the meadow, the ground opens up to reveal a silver-red staircase. The stepmother and her daughters hurry down the steps, anticipating a great fortune at the bottom, only to have the ground swallow them up, sealing their fate. Sylva retrieves the silver ribbon lying on the grass and presses it to her bosom. Years later, after she is married and has children of her own, she bequeaths it to her daughter.

Another fairy tale rooted in feminist sensibilities is Jeanne Desy's *The Princess Who Stood on Her Own Two Feet*. In Desy's tale, the villain is not a wicked stepmother but a crass and insensitive prince. Unlike other contemporary fairy tales that draw their inspiration from classical sources, *The Princess Who Stood on Her Own Two Feet* relies on its own story line. Like the princess in its title, the tale stands on its own two feet.

The princess in Desy's story is beautiful, intelligent, and possessed of many talents. Not only can she easily tally the contents of the royal treasury on an abacus, but she is able to master any subject presented to her by the royal tutors. In addition to her intellectual prowess, she is artistically inclined: she plays the zither with ease and also designs exquisite tapestries. She also happens to be very tall. The only thing the princess lacks is love, for there is no man in the kingdom who is a suitable match.

The princess does, however, have an affectionate companion, a golden-haired Afghan hound with thin, aristocratic features who was given to her by a friendly wizard. Faithful and true, the animal keeps the princess company during the day and sleeps at the foot of her bed at night. But the princess is the first to admit, "a dog is a dog and not a prince." And the princess longs to be wed.

One day a prince from a neighboring kingdom is sent by his parents to propose a marriage alliance with the princess that will benefit both kingdoms. A betrothal feast is arranged, and the princess nearly swoons in her chair when she sets eyes on the prince. He is more handsome and dashing than she ever imagined. So delighted is she to have him as her prospective husband that she spends the entire feast holding hands with him under the banquet table.

After the meal is over, it is time for dancing. The royal troubadours take out their instruments and begin to play a waltz. The prince asks the princess to honor him by dancing the first dance, and she rises to accept his invitation. But the moment she stands up, a great shadow passes over his face. The prince stares at the princess in disbelief.

"What is it?" she cried. But the prince would not speak, and dashed from the hall.

For a long time the princess studied her mirror that night, wondering what the prince had seen.

"If you could talk," she said to the dog, "you could tell me, I know it," for the animal's eyes were bright and intelligent. "What did I do wrong?"

The dog, in fact, could talk; it's just that nobody had ever asked him anything before.

"You didn't do anything," he said, "it's your height."

"My height?" the princess cries out in astonishment. "But I am a princess. I'm supposed to be tall." She points out that height is part of her royal heritage, and that everyone in the royal family is tall. But the dog explains to her that while that might be true, men from other kingdoms like to be taller than their wives.

"But why?" the princess asks. The dog fumbles for an answer but cannot come up with one. It makes as little sense to him as it does the princess.

SHIFTS IN THE POWER BALANCE BETWEEN MEN AND WOMEN

The matter of height, of course, is a metaphor for the power differences between men and women. The prince cannot tolerate a wife who is taller than he, for it suggests that she may eclipse him. He cannot even bear to discuss the matter. Perhaps he doesn't fully understand it himself. All he knows is that her height disturbs him, so much so that he calls off the wedding and returns home.

The princess really doesn't understand the reason for the prince's departure but wants to set things right. She rushes to the wizard and asks whether he can make her shorter. The wizard sadly explains that such a feat is not within his power. He can make the princess fatter or thinner, even change her into a raven, but he cannot do anything about her height. Despondent and depressed, the princess takes to her bed.

Meanwhile, the king and queen have convinced the prince to reconsider his decision and to give the match another chance. He agrees and returns to the castle, where the princess is languishing in her bedroom. Standing by her bedside, he naturally towers over the princess, thereby rekindling his earlier attraction to her.

The prince notices that the princess has become pale from lying indoors so long and offers to take her out for some fresh air. He invites her to go horseback riding, for on a horse, as in a chair, the princess is no taller than he. But during the ride the princess's horse stumbles and throws her to the ground. When the prince assists her to her feet, he once again is reminded of how much taller she is than he.

The princess sees the displeasure in his face and immediately crumples to the ground, crying out, "My legs, I cannot stand." The prince picks her up and carries her back to her room, his chest puffed up with manly pride. Since she cannot stand, he once again looms over her.

The princess spends the next few weeks in bed "recuperating." But she finds herself increasingly bored as the days go by. It's not the most pleasant thing in the world for an energetic and talented young woman to be cooped up in her room all day.

Since she was often idle now, the princess practiced witty and amusing sayings. She meant only to please the prince, but he turned on her after one particularly subtle and clever remark and said sharply, "Haven't you ever heard that women should be seen and not heard?"

The princess sank into thought. She didn't quite understand the saying, but she sensed that it was somehow like her tallness. For just as he preferred her sitting, not standing, he seemed more pleased when she listened, and more remote when she talked.

THE PRINCESS SACRIFICES TO APPEASE THE PRINCE

The princess decides to stop talking, once again sacrificing her pride in order to placate the prince. She communicates her wishes on a slate to him and to her servants, but late at night, when no one is around, she satisfies her need to engage in intelligent conversation by conversing with her faithful dog.

The prince is less than satisfied with this arrangement. He is annoyed by the affection the princess lavishes on the animal. The dog senses his days are numbered and says as much to the princess. When she tells him she doesn't know what she would do without him, he replies, "You'd better get used to the idea. The prince doesn't like me." And so saying, he slumps to the floor and dies, sacrificing himself for the princess's happiness.

The grief-stricken princess is inconsolable. She wraps her faithful companion in the folds of her dress and sets out to bury him. On the way to the grave site, she is intercepted by the prince, who callously remarks, "I thought you got rid of that thing weeks ago."

"What you call 'this thing,'" the princess tells him, "died to spare me pain. And I intend to bury him with honor."

The prince is surprised to hear the princess speak and comments on the fact that she is talking.

"Yes," she smiles, looking down on him. "I'm talking. The better to tell you good-bye. So good-bye." That might have been the end of it, but when her mother, the queen, hears what happened, she becomes agitated.

"Well, my dear," the queen said that night, when the princess appeared in the throne room. "You've made a proper mess of things. We have allegiances to think of. I'm sure you're aware of the very complex negotiations you have quite ruined. Your duty as a princess . . ."

"It is not necessarily my duty to sacrifice everything," the princess interrupted. "And I have other duties: a princess says what she thinks. A princess stands on her own two feet. A princess stands tall. And she does not betray those who love her." Her royal parents did not reply. But they seemed to ponder her words.

That night the princess slips out of the castle to visit the grave of her beloved pet. Standing by the grave site, she considers all she has given up for love.

"How foolish we are," she says aloud. "For a stupid prince, I let my wise companion die." She places a white rose on the grave and waters it with a silver watering can.

THE HAPPY ENDING

On her way back to the castle gate, she hears a noise in the dark and looks up to see a handsome horseman. The rider has long golden hair and aristocratic features, and she senses that he could be a prince. She notices that his banner is a white rose on a black background. The princess asks if he can lower it so that she can examine it more closely. He brings the banner close to her face.

"Death," she breathed.

"No, no," he said smiling. "Rebirth. And for that, a death is sometimes necessary." He dismounted and bent to kiss the princess's hand. She breathed a tiny prayer as he straightened up, but it was not answered. Indeed, he was several inches shorter than she was. The princess straightened her spine.

"It is a pleasure to look up to a proud and beautiful lady," the young prince said, and his large eyes spoke volumes. The princess blushed.

"We're still holding hands," she said foolishly. The elegant prince smiled, and kept hold of her hand, and they went toward the castle.

HEROINES MAKE BETTER CHOICES

Stories like *The Moon Ribbon* and *The Princess Who Stood on Her Own Two Feet* use a fairy-tale format to suggest ways in which stereotyped images of women—and men—can be reshaped through fantasy. A fairy tale need not feature a passive heroine, a savior prince, or a malevolent older woman to make sense, although many contemporary tales still include a witch. The heroines in these stories have a sense of humor, actively establish themselves as free-thinking individuals, and, most important, make choices that serve their own interests. In Judith Viorst's abbreviated rendering of the Cinderella story entitled ... *And Then the Prince Knelt Down and Tried to Put the Glass Slipper on Cinderella's Foot,* the heroine takes a second look at the prince when he arrives at her door with the glass slipper. In the clear light of day, she notices he has a funny nose and is not nearly as dashing as he looked the night of the ball. Quickly deciding he is not for her, she pretends the slipper is too tight and thus cannot get her foot into it. Like the princess who stood on her own two feet, Viorst's Cinderella and other fairy-tale heroines of the future may decide to satisfy their own desires rather than allowing themselves to become the object of someone else's. They may weigh the options available to them, and not be blindly swept away by considerations that in the long run may not be self-fulfilling.

Fairy Tales Are an Ideal Literary Form

C.S. Lewis

C.S. Lewis made it quite clear that in writing his best loved series, *The Chronicles of Narnia*, he did not set out to write children's literature. Rather, he was drawn to the peculiar form of the fairy tale and saw here an opportunity to convey Christian values and his faith in God. In the following article, Lewis describes his attraction to the simplicity and directness of the fairy tale form, both as an artist and as a man with an interest in saying something of substance in his creative works. He believed that fairy tales, above all other literary forms, were best suited to creating a receptivity or openness in the minds of readers, whereby they might experience something beyond what the rational and guarded mind might normally admit. C.S. Lewis (1898–1963) was born in Ireland and is known for his novels, literary criticism and theological writings in addition to his well known works for children.

In the sixteenth century when everyone was saying that poets (by which they meant all imaginative writers) ought 'to please and instruct', [Italian Renaissance poet, Torquato] Tasso made a valuable distinction. He said that the poet, as poet, was concerned solely with pleasing. But then every poet was also a man and a citizen; in that capacity he ought to, and would wish to, make his work edifying as well as pleasing.

Now I do not want to stick very close to the renaissance ideas of 'pleasing' and 'instructing'. Before I could accept either term it might need so much redefining that what was left of it at the end would not be worth retaining. All I want to use is the distinction between the author as author and the author as man, citizen, or Christian. What this comes to for me is that there are usually two reasons for writing an imaginative work, which may be called Author's reason and the Man's. If only one of these is present, then, so far as I am concerned, the book will not be written. If the first is lacking, it can't; if the second is lacking, it shouldn't.

In the Author's mind there bubbles up every now and then the material for a story. For me it invariably begins with mental pictures. This ferment leads to nothing unless it is accompanied with the longing for a Form: verse or prose, short story, novel, play or what not. When these two things click you have the Author's impulse complete. It is now a thing inside him pawing to get out. He longs to see that bubbling stuff pouring into that Form as the housewife longs to see the new jam pouring into the clean jam jar. This nags him all day long and gets in the way of his work and his sleep and his meals. It's like being in love.

While the Author is in this state, the Man will of course have to criticize the proposed book from quite a different point of view. He will ask how the gratification of this impulse will fit in with all the other things he wants, and ought to do or be. Perhaps the whole thing is too frivolous and trivial (from the Man's point of view, not the Author's) to justify the time and pains it would involve. Perhaps it would be unedifying when it was done. Or else perhaps (at this point the Author cheers up) it looks like being 'good', not in a merely literary sense, but 'good' all around.

This may sound rather complicated but it is really very like what happens about other things. You are attracted by a girl; but is she the sort of girl you'd be wise, or right, to marry? You would like to have lobster for lunch; but does it agree with you and is it wicked to spend that amount of money on a meal? The Author's impulse is a desire (it is very like an itch), and of course, like every other desire, needs to be criticized by the whole Man.

Let me now apply this to my own fairy tales. Some people seem to think that I began by asking myself how I could say something about Christianity to children; then fixed on the fairy tale as an instrument; then collected information about child-psychology and decided what age group I'd write for; then drew up a list of basic Christian truths and hammered out 'allegories' to embody them. This is all pure moonshine. I couldn't write in that way at all. Everything began with images; a faun carrying an umbrella, a queen on a sledge, a magnificent lion. At first there wasn't even anything Christian about them; that element pushed itself in of its own accord. It was part of the bubbling.

THE APPEAL OF THE FAIRY TALE FORM

Then came the Form. As these images sorted themselves into events (i.e., became a story) they seemed to demand no love interest and no close psychology. But the Form which excludes these things is the fairy tale. And the moment I thought of that I fell in love with the Form itself: its brevity, its severe restraints on description, its flexible traditionalism, its inflexible hostility to all analysis, digression, reflections and 'gas'. I was now enamoured of it. Its very limitations of vocabulary became an attraction; as the hardness of the stone pleases the sculptor or the difficulty of the sonnet delights the sonneteer.

On that side (as Author) I wrote fairy tales because the Fairy Tale seemed the ideal Form for the stuff I had to say.

Then of course the Man in me began to have his turn. I thought I saw how stories of this kind could steal past a certain inhibition which had paralysed much of my own religion in childhood. Why did one find it so hard to feel as one was told one ought to feel about God or about the sufferings of Christ? I thought the chief reason was that one was told one ought to. An obligation to feel can freeze feelings. And reverence itself did harm. The whole subject was associated with lowered voices; almost as if it were something medical. But supposing that by casting all these things into an imaginary world, stripping them of their stained-glass and Sunday school associations, one could make them for the first time appear in their real potency? Could one not thus steal past those watchful dragons? I thought one could.

That was the Man's motive. But of course he could have done nothing if the Author had not been on the boil first.

FAIRY TALES FOR ALL AGES

You will notice that I have throughout spoken of Fairy Tales, not 'children's stories'. Professor J. R. R. Tolkien in [his essay "On Fairy-Stories"] has shown that the connection between fairy tales and children is not nearly so close as publishers and educationalists think. Many children don't like them and many adults do. The truth is, as he says, that they are now associated with children because they are out of fashion with adults; have in fact retired to the nursery as old furniture used to retire there, not because the children had begun to like it but because their elders had ceased to like it.

I was therefore writing 'for children' only in the sense that I excluded what I thought they would not like or understand; not in the sense of writing what I intended to be below adult attention. I may of course have been deceived, but the principle at least saves one from being patronizing. I never wrote down to anyone; and whether the opinion condemns or acquits my own work, it certainly is my opinion that a book worth reading only in childhood is not worth reading even then. The inhibitions which I hoped my stories would overcome in a child's mind may exist in a grown-up's mind too, and may perhaps be overcome by the same means.

The Fantastic or Mythical is a Mode available at all ages for some readers; for others, at none. At all ages, if it is well used by the author and meets the right reader, it has the same power: to generalize while remaining concrete, to present in palpable form not concepts or even experiences but whole classes of experience, and to throw off irrelevancies. But at its best it can do more; it can give us experiences we have never had and thus, instead of 'commenting on life', can add to it. I am speaking, of course, about the thing itself, not my own attempts at it.

'Juveniles', indeed! Am I to patronize sleep because children sleep sound? Or honey because children like it?

CHAPTER 5

Assessment of the Genre

Fairy Tales Promote Self-Discovery

Bruno Bettelheim

In his classic work *The Uses of Enchantment: The Meaning and Importance of Fairy Tales,* child psychiatrist Bruno Bettelheim says that fairy tales, like no other literary form, can effectively promote a sense of meaning and purpose in the life of severely disturbed children. Fairy tales directly confront the most serious existential dilemmas—the need to be loved, to have a sense of worth, the love of life and fear of death—in a way the child can readily absorb. In the following article, Bettelheim describes fairy tales as metaphors for the dangerous journey on the path to greater self knowledge. "Hansel and Gretel" and "Jack and the Beanstalk" explore the confrontation of one's deepest fears, and the ensuing victory and rise to a richer, more meaningful existence.

[German Poet Rainer Maria] Rilke describes what forms the essence of great art: "Beauty is nothing but the beginning of terror we are still just able to bear, and why we adore it so is because it serenely disdains to destroy us." This certainly is true for the better of those traditional folk tales which, with a regrettable misnomer, we call fairy tales. Their beauty is inextricably interwoven with the terror they arouse and the hero's—and with it our rescue—at the happy ending. Fairy tales present to us this essence of beauty in a most concise manner, and in ways in which it can be comprehended even by the most naive peruser of this literature, even by the young child.

Beginning in a setting akin to our most ordinary existence, fairy tales take us in a short and dramatic move to the very edge of the abyss, as does any true exploration of the meaning of life, of its deeper purpose, as does any serious

Excerpted from "Fairy Tales as Ways of Knowing," by Bruno Bettelheim in *Fairy Tales as Ways of Knowing: Essays on Marchen in Psychology, Society, and Literature,* edited by Michael M. Metzger and Katherine Mommsen. Copyright © 1981 by Peter Lang Publishers, Ltd. Reprinted with permission from Peter Lang Publishers.

effort to know ourselves that penetrates beyond the surface of our being and reaches into the darkest recesses of our mind, particularly into those to the impact of which we try to close ourselves, which we desire not to recognize. These are the aspects of our existence which threaten us most, which are likely to cause our troubles but which also endow our existence with some of its deepest meaning. This darkness within ourselves is what we need most to become acquainted with if we want to know ourselves. The fairy tale, after having made us tremble by taking us to the edge of the abyss, after having forced us to face evil and all the darkness which also resides within us, after having acquainted us with what we rather wish to avoid, serenely rescues us. In the course of the story we gain the ability to live a richer and more meaningful life on a much higher plane than the one in which we found ourselves at the story's beginning, where the hero, who is our mirror image, was forced to embark on his perilous voyage of self-discovery.

HÄNSEL AND GRETEL LEARN THEY CAN DEFEAT THE WITCH

Hänsel and Gretel are two very ordinary children when we meet them at the beginning of their story. Like most children, in the darkness of night they are assailed by anxious fantasies about their parents' planning to get rid of them, are beset by starvation anxiety. Convinced that they can not take care of themselves, they know only one way to be safe: to hang on most determinedly to what they are most familiar with: their home, mother's apron strings. But it will no longer do. Like all children, Hänsel and Gretel must learn not only to become able to fend for themselves, but also to meet the dark aspects of life. Most of all they must learn to combat victoriously their primitive anxieties about being starved and devoured which are closely connected with their deep oral cravings which tempt them to eat up even what seems to offer most pleasant shelter, symbolized by the gingerbread house. They will not be able to be themselves and to meet the world successfully unless they have first faced courageously their anxious fantasy of the archetypical bad, the devouring mother, and freed themselves of it. It is an image which each child creates out of his experience that he wishes to eat up his mother so that she will never be able to desert him even for a moment; and his fear that, in retaliation, the mother will eat him up. It is an image as old as the child's nursing experience when, as he sucks from the breast—or from the bottle which he experiences as a poor substitute for the breast—he imagines himself as incorporating the mother. It is the fear of the bad mother which is the inescapable reverse image of the loving mother, the counterpart of the giving and protective mother which replaces her image when she also makes demands and criticizes the infant. It is the consequence of the infant's utter dependence on an all powerful person, the intentions of whom one can not fathom and which therefore may be evil. All this is symbolically expressed in the fairy tale by the juxtaposition of the all good mother who gave birth to the child but soon disappeared, to be replaced by the demanding and frustrating stepmother, as in Cinderella.

Hänsel and Gretel come face to face with these their fantasies about the devouring mother as they encounter them in the form of the witch. This witch hides within, or behind the alluring, the wishfulfilling oral fantasy of the gingerbread house, which has its origin in the earliest phase of the child's development, when he experiences everything in terms of his orality. This archetypical image of the bad mother we met at the story's beginning in its more ordinary form of the depriving and rejecting stepmother who is intent on forcing the children to learn to shift for themselves, to stop being a burden to their parents, to begin to become masters of their fate. As reluctant as the children are to do so, the fairy tale tells that they will perish unless they become able to do so. Harsh events force them to learn to defeat evil incarnate: the witch. In destroying her they free themselves at the same time from dependence on their orality, and learn to activate and with it to recognize the forces of self protection which reside in them. This they do as they overcome their fear of the all destructive figure of the witch, outwit her, and in the end overcome her.

Because Hänsel and Gretel were able to gain control over their nightmarish terror—given tangible form in the figure of the witch—they gained confidence in their own strength to defeat evil and to rescue themselves. Because they succeeded in their battle against the primordial oral anxiety about being devoured, their lives are as if miraculously enriched. This is symbolically expressed by their gaining the witch's jewels which henceforth provide them with a secure livelihood. Having found their own strength and gained the ability to exercise it, they no longer need to live in fear, nor to depend on others for their well-being. Life will be good for them forever after.

ACCESSING THE HIGHER SELF

It was their experience in the dark and pathless forest, it was their successful encounter with terror which did all this for them. Finding oneself in a dark, impenetrable forest is an ancient literary image for man in need of gaining self knowledge. Dante evoked it at the beginning of the *Divine Comedy*, but long before him it served as image of man in search of himself, of man caught in a moral crisis, of man having to meet a developmental impasse as he wishes to move from a lower to a higher level of self-consciousness. It is the ambience where Hänsel and Gretel meet the witch. It is the ambience into which the knight errant rides out, seeking the greatest adventure man can encounter: to meet and to find himself, as he does battle against the forces of evil. This evil, this darkness that surrounds him in the forest, is but a projection of the darkness that resides in himself, and so is the dragon against which he does battle. The dragon is a figment of his imagination into which he projected all that he can not accept in himself. By defeating him he wins a moral victory over himself, symbolized by his rescuing the dragon's victim. His victory is gaining permanent access to his higher self which up to then had been kept captive, inoperative, by the powers of darkness. Because of their encounter with the witch, Hänsel and Gretel's childish naiveté and utter dependence on others is replaced by a proud maturity which permits them not only to rescue themselves but also their father, who had despaired of his ability to take care of his children. The children, who at the story's beginning had felt themselves the helpless pawns of their parents and of fate, at its end are masters of their destiny, and able to take care of their parent. What happier ending to a story can there be?

HONORING INDIVIDUALITY

Taking in, comprehending what a fairy tale reveals in symbolic form about how one must organize one's life to master the difficulties one invariably encounters, requires not only a repeated listening to the tale, but also a chance to ponder its meaning to one's heart's delight. Only then can the child begin to understand that he can not remain forever dependent, can not expect all his life to be taken care of by others; only then does the child comprehend the shortcomings of relying for his security on his parents, recognize the advantages of becoming a person in his own right. Only then does he gain hope that however nightmarishly difficult it may seem to him to become truly himself, it is a task he can master and be much the better for it. It is a lesson that many fairy tales teach, each in its own and different form, by means of different images appropriate to the particular problem it presents in symbolic form and in an esthetic rendering suitable to it; and to the story's specific content.

JACK DISCOVERS INNER STRENGTHS

The images which *Jack and the Beanstalk* evokes are neither parents who plan to desert their children, nor children being lost in a deep, dark forest with no way out. But the essential topic is, as always, an event which requires a courageous meeting of one's fate. This Jack must do, as must every hero of a fairy tale.

As long as the good cow Milky White gave milk, Jack's life was pleasant, uneventful, without challenges, but also without growth, without offering him a chance to develop his initiative, to become himself. All this changes overnight when Milky White stops giving the milk which up to then sustained Jack's life. This stopping of the supply of the life-giving milk is an image much closer to the twofold origins of starvation anxiety, which are the fear of the infant that mother will stop nursing him, and the real experience of his being weaned, whether he likes it or not. Jack's fateful encounter, which pitches him into battle against the projections of his anxieties, is not one with a witch in a forest, but with a giant in the sky.

While his mother thought him foolish for exchanging the cow for some bean seeds, and punished him for having trusted his feelings for what was a good exchange, up in the sky he finds an understanding mother figure who protects him, and thus permits him to gain what he needs both for his survival, and for becoming a real person. Thanks to her he brings back from his excursion into the sky, which he had reached by climbing up on his magic beanstalk, what replaces the cow as providing for his and his mother's livelihood: a bag of gold.

For the good life, for achieving independence, for becoming an autonomous person, it is not sufficient to acquire a bag of gold. Eventually it will be spent, and one will be without means of subsistence as one was when Milky White stopped giving milk. Taking from others is no way to be independent. The goose which lays the golden eggs symbolizes the next step in Jack's growing up: he has learned that just spending is not enough, one must also be able to replenish what one expends. If one does, one has learned to provide oneself with the essentials for living. But even so, it is still a life without purpose. To become a good life, it must also be invested with higher purposes, such as esthetic experiences. These are symbolized by the anxiety that the child may be devoured.

But the story does not end with Jack having gained the golden harp. The ogre pursues him, using the same magic pathway, the magic beanstalk, which permitted Jack his excursions into the world of wishfulfilling and at the same time terrifying fantasies. As the ogre pursues Jack down the beanstalk, he cries for his mother to cut it down. But she knows that doing this for Jack will not free him from seeking magic solutions to life's real problems. This only he can do as he realizes that living in the world of wishfulfilling fantasies only ends up in catastrophe. So she hands him the ax with which he chops off the beanstalk, depriving himself of any further reliance on magic solutions to life's real problems at the same time as he frees himself of those anxious fantasies of being devoured or otherwise destroyed which are the inescapable consequence of relying on others to provide one with what one needs for oneself.

SECURITY RESIDES WITHIN

Typical for this, as for all true fairy tales, is that the child or adolescent hero has to meet fearful dangers and to engage in actions requiring great valor before he can gain his rewards. However the hero may have been threatened as the story unfolds, in the end he is rescued. This is even true for stories in which the child is killed and dismembered, as in the Brothers Grimm's story "The Juniper Tree", in which the child is not only killed, but made into a black pudding, and eaten by his father; or for stories in which the child is devoured by an animal, as in Red Riding Hood. The eventual rescue, complete restoration, and the elevation of the child hero to a superior existence, this is the mark of the true folk fairy tale. Its purpose is not only to make us acquainted with the facts that life is difficult and entails often dangerous struggles, but also that only through the mastery of succeeding crises in our existence can we eventually find our true self. Having achieved it, we then need no longer to live in fear because we have gained true security which resides not in others but only in ourselves. At the end, the fairy tale dismisses us with a positive outlook on life, based on the conviction that evil will be punished, and the good will be rewarded.

Fairy Tales Send the Wrong Message

Robert Moore

According to Robert Moore, many famous fairy tales are based on antiquated values and proffer negative and dysfunctional role models to readers. Heroines are passive, useless, and dependent on their physical beauty to lure men to their rescue. Male figures often commit reprehensible acts with no consequence. Materialism, elitism, and a subtle racist bias pervade the classical tales. A "happily ever after" ending is secured through magic, luck, or some external source, rather than personal initiative. To counter these damaging images, Moore says it is incumbent upon parents and educators to teach children to critically assess what they read. Moore was resource coordinator at the Racist and Sexist Resource Center for Educators when he wrote the article.

Traditionally, it has been thought that fairy tales are an important literary experience for children: they are exciting, satisfy children's boundless imaginations and provide useful lessons and morals. But an analysis of the images and values that fairy tales are transmitting reveals serious flaws in the quality of that literary experience.

The "classic" fairy tales that are so popular in America are almost all of European origin, reflecting the cultural and economic values and attitudes of white, western people. Western societies have undergone great changes since these tales were written. However, the societies' values and beliefs and the behaviors that derive from them have not changed appreciably, even though many of them are now obsolete and dysfunctional. To the extent that fairy tales are part of the socialization process, they encourage or reinforce concepts

Excerpted from "From Rags to Witches: Stereotypes, Distortions, and Anti-Humanism in Fairy Tales," by Robert Moore, *Interracial Books for Children Bulletin*, 1975.

and behaviors that are being questioned increasingly by concerned educators and parents.

Most adults regard fairy tales as fantasy or satire. Arbuthnot and Sutherland, in *Children and Books,* write that in "The Princess and the Pea," Hans Christian Andersen takes "as sly a jibe at snobbery and the myths of blue-bloodedness as can be found anywhere." The editors of *Anthology of Children's Literature* state that:

> The proof he uses to show why the princess is a "real" one reflects the feelings of the poor shoemaker's son toward the higher ranks of the social order. This modern fairy tale could have been created only by one who had learned from experience how stupid is the basis of superiority which the so-called highest classes appropriate to themselves.

The problem is that children usually take these stories at face value, making no distinction between fantasy and reality. Arbuthnot and Sutherland admit this: "Most of the entire goes over the children's heads, and they take the stories literally. They are perfectly serious over the absurd princess on her twenty mattressess."

UNASSERTIVE HEROINES

One of the most obvious and pervasive negative aspects of fairy tales is their sex-role stereotyping. Females are usually portrayed as princesses or poor girls on their way to becoming princesses, fairy godmothers or good fairies, wicked and evil witches, jealous and spiteful sisters, proud, vain and hateful stepmothers, or shrewish wives. Beauty is the dominant attribute of "good" women, their main strength and saving grace. The most powerful and enterprising women are usually evil—either witches, mean stepmothers or jealous sisters who act independently and, for a time (until thwarted by a male), with effect. Aggressiveness or the power to solve their problems is not often assigned to "good" females. Schemes against the beautiful and virtuous heroine are foiled not by the heroine herself, but by a magic godmother or, more often, a male in the form of a handsome prince or mystical dwarf.

Red Riding Hood and her grandmother are saved from death by a hunter. Snow White is also saved from death by a hunter and is then assisted by dwarfs who give her shelter and a handsome prince who brings her back to life. The females in "Rumpelstiltskin" and "Snow-White and Rose-Red" are also rescued from their predicaments by males—in the first instance by a dwarf, and in the second by a prince disguised as a bear. Cinderella is helped by another woman—her fairy godmother—but in the end it is her beauty that overcomes her problems and a prince who snatches her from the jaws of fate.

Gretel is one of the few females who defeats an evil character without the intervention of magic, mysticism or a male. But, for most of the story, Gretel is frightened and tearful in the face of adversity and in need of comfort and support from her brother Hansel—who is strong, intelligent and brave. Forced to act when Hansel is locked up and unable to take the lead, she finally asserts herself by pushing the witch into the oven. One wishes Hansel were on the scene, yet passive, while Gretel acts decisively to save them both.

Another female who is relatively assertive and adventurous (but underneath, an "old fashioned gal") is the princess in "The Iron Stove." When a prince is imprisoned in a stove by an old witch, the princess—who is lost in the forest—comes upon the stove. The prince begs her to help him get free and offers, as a reward, to marry her—sight unseen! Thinking only that she has stumbled upon a talking stove, the princess says (uncharacteristically for a female character), "Good Heavens! What can I do with an iron stove?" She finally agrees to help the prince—a positive female action—but only because she is lost and needs *his* help to get home. When she peeps in the stove, she sees that he is "a youth so handsome and so brilliant with gold and with precious jewels, that her very soul was delighted." After the prince is freed, "He wanted to take her away with him to his kingdom, but she entreated" him to let her see her father once again. Failing to follow his instructions, she becomes separated from him and embarks on a lonely, treacherous journey to find him. She crosses a slippery glass mountain, three piercing swords and a great lake (all with the magic assistance of toads) only to find that the prince "had another woman by his side whom he wanted to marry" because he thought the princess was dead. So far, the princess has had an unusually exciting experience for a female character. But it must be remembered that she was "hanging in there" mainly to fulfill that most important of female needs—a man.

Her harrowing escapades culminate in a classic contest between two women for the attention of a man. The wily princess, sensing the "female" weaknesses of her adversary, entices the new maiden with beautiful dresses. She then persuades the new maiden to allow her to sleep in the prince's bed three times (to let him know she is still alive). Each time the maiden "gave her permission because the dress was so pretty, and she had never had one like it." The maiden does not, however, value dresses more than men, for each time she puts the prince to sleep for the night with sleeping powder. . . . Enough! The plot may seem murky but the stereotyped behaviors are crystal clear.

BEAUTY IS ALL

A great many fairy tale heroines are defined almost solely by physical appearances—that is, their beauty. Although many of these women are kind and display perseverance (or is it acquiescence?), it is their beauty, not personality or actions, that defines them and makes them valuable to others. "Beauty and the Beast," "Snow White," "Sleeping Beauty," "Rumpelstiltskin," "Snow-White and Rose-Red" and "Puss in Boots" all feature beautiful women whose fulfillment is derived from handsome men and/or princes and from marriage (or, as it is put in "The Princess and the Pea," being "taken as his wife"). With the possible exception of the women in "Beauty and the Beast" and "Snow-White and Rose-Red," who show compassion for "creatures" (soon-to-be handsome princes), all other women are passive, empty and dependent. (Actually, Beauty's behavior towards her father could more rightly be described as self-sacrificing, a standard female "virtue.")

Women characters are often introduced as secondary and inferior people, or as possessions of men. "Hansel and Gretel" begins: "Close to a large forest lived a woodcutter, with his wife and his two children." "Rumpelstiltskin" begins: "There once was a miller who was very poor, but he had a beautiful daughter." "Cinderella" begins: "There once was an honest gentleman who took for his second wife the proudest and most disagreeable lady in the whole country." The prince in "The Princess and the Pea" looks for a princess as one might shop for a new car—he "wanted to find himself a princess. But, of course, she would have to be a real, genuine princess." Unfortunately, it was "hard to tell whether they were the real thing or not" so he returned home disappointed. As luck would have it, he finally found a "real genuine one" and "took her for his wife." An illustration with the LeGallienne translation portrays princesses begging and pleading like puppies in a pet shop to be "taken" by him.

Female roles are very traditional—those of mother, wife and housewife. The dwarfs ask Snow White to live with them: " 'You could sew and mend, and keep everything tidy.' This made Snow White very happy: 'Oh, thank you,' she said, 'I could want nothing better.' " (Not only is she more than satisfied with this traditional assignment, but she takes absolutely no action against her stepmother who tried to have her killed and is the cause of her banishment.)

PREFERRED TREATMENT FOR MALES

Males (human or animal) are usually courageous, adventurous, powerful, intelligent and resourceful. "Puss in Boots" is creative and industrious. Jack (of Beanstalk fame) is daring, courageous and resourceful in defeating the giant and saving his mother and himself from poverty. The bear (prince) in "Snow-White and Rose-Red" acts decisively to defeat the evil dwarf. Hansel is brave, resourceful and intelligent, as well as being an emotional pillar of strength for Gretel to lean on. The most adventurous thing Red Riding Hood does is to dawdle and pick flowers on her way to grandmother's, after her mother has told her not to tarry. (Picking flowers is a very passive activity and one that Snow-White and Rose-Red engage in frequently when they are not cleaning house.) The only consequence of Riding Hood's flower-picking is that it gives the wolf time to beat her to grandmother's house. Yet, after being saved by the hunter, she concludes: "I will never again wander off into the forest for as long as I live, when my mother forbids it." Riding Hood has learned her lesson well: Wandering—for girls—is a no-no. Meanwhile, Jack will continue to wander where and whenever he likes, slaying giants as he goes.

Other men, while not necessarily adventurous or powerful, are still portrayed more favorably than their female counterparts, who are evil, hateful, scornful, shrewish or cruel. In "The Fisherman and His Wife," the fisherman is portrayed as modest and goodhearted while his wife is domineering and greedy.

Hansel and Gretel's father loves them dearly and only abandons them in the woods because of their mean stepmother. The stepmother dies in the end, and the father is thrilled at his children's return. Cinderella's father is a good man who is completely at the mercy of his hateful wife and spiteful daughters. The father of the prince who awakens Sleeping Beauty is, at worst, a neutral character, while his wife is a child-eating ogre. Beauty, of "Beauty and the Beast" has a father and brothers who are decent and love her; her sisters are jealous and hateful.

Even men who do negative things often have redeeming virtues or, at any rate, are not admonished for their negative behavior. Hansel and Gretel's father suffers only temporarily for his deeds and is rewarded by getting his children back—plus a small fortune. The soldier in "The Tinder Box" kills a witch after she provides him with great wealth, kills a king and queen in order to have their daughter (a beautiful princess, of course) and ends up a king himself, with the daughter as his queen ("which pleased her very much"). When the poor father in "Rumpelstiltskin" lies to the king about his daughter's ability to spin straw into gold, he gets her into all sorts of predicaments but is never admonished for his actions—in fact, because of them, his daughter becomes queen. The greedy king in the same story threatens the woman with death if she does not produce more gold, then decides to marry her "Even if she is only a miller's daughter [for] I shan't find a richer woman in the whole world" (she is also beautiful). He ends up with the gold, the beautiful woman and nary a hassle.

QUESTIONABLE VALUES

On the surface, several tales seem relevant for children today because they do not project the two-parent nuclear family of "Dick and Jane" fame. Snow-White and Rose-Red live with their poor, widowed mother; Jack lives with his poor, widowed mother, and others are into second marriages (Cinderella's father, Snow White's father, Hansel and Gretel's father). However, the single mothers are invariably meek and incapable of supporting their families, except in poverty. Moreover, while Jack's boldness and courage save him and his mother, Snow-White and Rose-Red make it possible for *their* mother to live "peacefully and happily" by marrying two princely brothers. As for second marriages, they are invariably a disaster, resolved only by the stepmother's death. In an age when a great number of children are experiencing single parentage and re-marriages, these stories are not terribly encouraging.

Materialism is another value commonly found in many fairy tales. Young readers learn that money solves your problems and allows you to live happily ever after—with a handsome prince or beautiful princess thrown in. Perhaps the most obnoxious of these odes to materialism is "The Tinder Box," in which a soldier meets an "ugly, old" witch who makes him wealthy in exchange for retrieving her magic tinder box. Not satisfied with the riches, he kills the witch because she will not tell him what the box is for. Taking the money and the box, he goes on to lead a "merry" life—his money having enabled him not only to possess the best of everything, but to become a popular, "thorough gentleman." (In all fairness, it should be noted that he gives away a lot of money to the poor.) The only thing he lacks is the beautiful princess, and he "longed to be a prince, so that he might have her for his wife." After using the magic box to kill the king, queen and numerous soldiers, he is rewarded for his killing and greed by becoming king and marrying the princess (to the victor go the spoils). As mentioned earlier, the satirical dimension of fairy tales is not perceived by children, so the message of this and other stories is that m-o-n-e-y spells happiness—no matter how you get it.

MAGIC PROMOTES PASSIVITY

Fairy tales are sometimes scorned for their proverbial "They lived happily ever after" endings, which distort reality for youth. But a far more insidious aspect of the stories is the nature of the actions that enable the characters to live happily ever after. Arbuthnot and Sutherland, writing of "Cinderella" and "Snow White," state that:

> . . . they dramatize the story conflict of good and evil. And they reiterate the old verities that kindness and goodness will triumph over evil if they are backed by wisdom, wit and courage. These are basic truths we should like built into the depths of the child's consciousness; they are the folk tales' great contributions to the child's social consciousness.

However, it is not "wisdom, wit and courage" that usually allow fairy tale characters to prevail over adversity.

"Hansel and Gretel," "Rumpelstiltskin," "Jack and the Beanstalk," "Beauty and the Beast," "Puss in Boots," "Snow-White and Rose-Red" and "Cinderella" all have characters who begin the story in poverty or oppressed conditions, with no explanation provided as to the socio-economic causes of their condition. Poverty and oppression are either real for many youngsters reading the stories, or realities that more fortunate readers need to be aware of. Yet in each of the above stories it is beauty, good luck, magic or mysticism that frees the character from hard times. Almost never is a change in status the result of actions taken by the characters themselves to overcome their situation by confronting its causes. To instruct youth that beauty, good luck or magic (or for that matter "old varities" like kindness, goodness, wisdom, wit and courage) will "cure" injustice deters them from recognizing the necessity for action—and the power of collective action—to confront the institutional and social causes of poverty and oppression.

ELITISM IN FAIRY TALES

"The Ugly Duckling" suffers a great deal of hatred and prejudice and ends up a stronger being for his suffering. But he changes from being "ugly" to being "beautiful," rather than being accepted and appreciated for what he is. "It does not matter in the least," says the story, "having been born in a duckyard if only you come out of a swan's egg!" (This bit of elitist nonsense is similar to the racist message our culture teaches white people that even if you're poor, you're "acceptable" if you're white.) In the real world, black skin does not change into white skin, females do not change into males, "ugliness" (by whose standards?) does not become "beauty" except in the eyes of the beholder and poverty does not change miraculously into wealth.

The elitism which pervades fairy tales is due partly to the fact that, as a genre, they originated in 17th century France as amusement for members of the court. Subsequently, they become voguish among the upper classes throughout Europe. Hence, the tales' litany: People are handsome, beautiful and popular when dressed in fine clothes; can be good people even *though* from poor backgrounds; are "acceptable" only after proving that though born in a duckyard, they hatched from a swan's egg; and are clearly better people if wealthy or royal than of the working class. Regarding the last point, persons of royal birth seem to vastly outnumber working people as characters in fairy tales.

RACIAL BIAS

As noted earlier, most of the classic and popular fairy tales are of European origin and reflect European culture. They also have only white people as characters. Andersen wrote in "The Princess and the Pea" that the prince travelled "all over the world" to find a real princess, yet the LaGallienne translation contains an illustration of the prince encountering, in his world-wide travels, six princesses—all white! Since the civilizations of Africa, Asia and the Americas predate those of Europe and contain royalty and great wealth, and since white people represent less than a quarter of the world's population, such dashes of ethnocentrism and racism are particularly offensive.

The whiteness of fairy tales alone should cause us concern about their use in our multiracial society. This atmosphere is epitomized by the queen in "Snow White" wishing for and being blessed with "a lovely little daughter who had skin as white as snow." One wonders if the child would have been so well-received had she been a lovely little daughter with skin as black as coal. At a time when the positive connotations of "white" and negative connotations of "black" that are manifest in the English language are being challenged, it seems inappropriate to continue celebrating stories in which all of the beautiful and good women are fair and white. Fairy tales perpetuate the correlation between beauty/virtue and whiteness and the concept that black is ugly, evil and to be feared.

NEED FOR CRITICAL ANALYSIS

Some will still argue that the fantasy in fairy tales is a necessary part of a child's literary diet, that children should not be burdened with unpleasant realities but rather allowed to enjoy the so-called innocence of youth. But surely children can be entertained by stories which provide larger-than-life situations without at the same time being fed negative stereotypes and role models, subtle racism and gross distortions of reality.

Fairy tales, like much of western literature, contain many values and assumptions which reinforce unhealthy and destructive images for the reader. It is not enough to dismiss these negative elements as reflections of the times in which the stories were written because of the real influence they have on the attitudes, expectations and behavior of people in today's world. Concerned parents and educators should work to liberate homes and schools from such potentially destructive materials and to provide children with more progressive and equally enjoyable fare. However, since it is next to impossible to prevent children from being exposed to fairy tales, we need also to assist them in recognizing negative concepts and values and in developing the skills to analyze whatever they read. In this way, fairy tales or any of the other sexist, racist and anti-humanist materials that abound in their world can become important tools for imparting more positive values and concepts.

Fairy Tales Can Provide a Positive Social Vision

Marina Warner

In *From the Beast to the Blonde: On Fairy Tales and their Tellers,* Marina Warner describes ways fairy tales function in different contexts, depending on the intention of the storyteller. Although repressive regimes have used the genre to indoctrinate and manipulate, the fairy tale has more often been the vehicle for covert social protest, suggesting radical alternative visions under the guise of the innocent tales. Fairy tales have the capacity to unite societies and break down national and cultural boundaries. Warner asserts there is a practical dimension to the faculty of wonder, whereby fairy tales can suggest a vision for a new world order based on the essential optimism characteristic of the genre. Marina Warner writes fiction and criticism and lives in London.

Fairy tales often engage with issues of light and darkness— the plots represent struggles to distinguish enemies from friends, the normal from the monstrous, and the slant they take is by no means always enlightened. The tales often demonize others in order to proclaim the side of the teller good, right, powerful—and beautiful. Fairy tale's simple, even simplistic dualism can be and has been annexed to ugly ends: the Romantic revival of folk literature in Germany unwittingly heralded the Nazi claim that 'their' fairy tales were racially Aryan homegrown products; in former Yugoslavia, the different factions are using folklore as one more weapon in their civil strife, raising heroes from the past, singing old ballads as battle cries, performing folk dances to a cacophony of competing regional music. Folk tales powerfully shape national memory; their poetic versions intersect with history, and in the contemporary embattled quest for indigenous identity, underestimating their sway over values and attitudes can be as dangerous as ignoring changing historical realities. . . .

[And yet] the very territory of popular, anonymous story-telling has proved an arena of resistance to tyranny, as well as a site of reconciliation and reversal for ostracized and con-demned figures. Storytelling can act to face the objects of de-rision or fear and sometimes—not always—inspire tolerance and even fellow-feeling; it can realign allegiances and remap terrors. Storytellers can also break through the limits of per-mitted thought to challenge conventions; fairy tales . . . offer a way of putting questions, of testing the structure as well as guaranteeing its safety, of thinking up alternatives as well as living daily reality in an examined way. . . .

FAIRY TALES AND SOCIAL PROTEST

While fairy tales have shored up traditional aspirations (for fame and fortune, above all), they can also act as fifth columnists, burrowing from within, in the very act of cir-culating the lessons of the status quo. And because utopian ambitions beat strongly in the heart of fairy tale, many writers have hidden and hide under its guileless and ap-parently childish façade, have wrapped its cloak of unre-ality around them; adopting its traditional formal simplic-ities they have attempted to challenge received ideas and raise questions into the minds of their audience: protest and fairy tale have long been associated. In conditions of censorship—in Paris under Louis XIV as well as Prague before 1989—fantasies can lead the censor a merry dance. The writings of the French *précieuses* [female intellectuals] and their disciples like Marie-Jeanne L'Héritier and Marie-Catherine d'Aulnoy campaigned for women's eman-cipation; nineteenth- and early twentieth-century writers of both sexes also struggled to shape an egalitarian, com-munal, anti-materialist ethic, as [English essayist and critic John] Ruskin did with 'The King of the Golden River', [Scottish novelist and poet] George MacDonald in his *Princess* books and Frank L. Baum with *The Wizard of Oz* and its sequels. [Czech author and critic] Karel Čapek wrote against the rise of Fascism in the 1930s, shoring up the qualities of tolerance and mercy in his tender, comic, blithe shaggy-dog fairy tales, poking fun at greed and folly, bureaucrats and bullies. The Czech poet Miroslav Holub has described what pleasure it gave writers to trick the Communist system by encoding their dissidence in bafflingly innocuous images, of Cinderella and other irreproachable figures. Today, writers for children (and sometimes for adults, too) who draw on fairytale motifs and characters, like Terry Jones, Joan Aiken, Jane Yolen, Tove Jansson, Terry Pratchett, are conjuring up dream worlds as personally idealistic, as politically and socially contentious, and often as spiritedly wary and iconoclastic, as their more apparently sophisticated precursors, Erasmus, Voltaire and Swift. . . .

FAIRY TALES UNITE PEOPLE

[The work of Italo Calvino illustrates a further dimension to the reach and impact of fairy tales. He] began by writing, as a young communist, a realist novel about the partisans, *Il Sentiero dei nidi di ragno* (The Path to the Nests of Spiders), which appeared in 1947. The cultural politics of the nineteenth and early twentieth centuries had assumed that representing the interests of the people as well as communicating with them required a naturalistic, documentary mode—a print off life to demonstrate the heroism and the injustice of the common folk. But then Calvino became interested in folklore, and after he published his resonant collection *Fiabe Italiane*, the fruit of years of scavenging and collating and editing fairy tales from all over Italy, Calvino himself became a fabulist [writer of fairy tales]—he gave himself to a literature of dreaming rather than representation, and began to see the writer as a shaman who takes flight to another world. In his last series of lectures, he wrote:

> I am accustomed to consider literature a search for knowledge. In order to move onto existential ground, I have to think of literature as extended to anthropology and ethnology and mythology. Faced with the precarious existence of tribal life—drought, sickness, evil influences—the shaman responded by ridding his body of weight and flying to another world, another level of perception, where he could find the strength to change the face of reality.

Through fairy tales he had heard, he said, the voices of the people, he had discovered the knowledge of another way of being, the fruits of struggle and hope. Crucially, he had also discovered common ground on which the agnostic and literate mandarin like himself stood beside the unlettered worker. It is a very important discovery: that fairy tale and fantasy can unite societies, across barriers of all kinds.

Storytelling can act as a social binding agent—like the egg yolk which, mixed up with the different coloured powders, produces colours of a painting. A story like 'Rashin Coatie',

---

MINOR DESPOTS AND PARASITIC PRINCES

In the following extract from an article which appeared in the London Times *in 1955, the journalist describes the way the East German communist government, recognizing the powerful socializing impact of children's fairy tales, saw the need to modify well-known tales in their concern to indoctrinate their people with Marxist ideology.*

Most students of claptrap were unaware that there were such things as Marxist fairy stories; but there are, for it has just been decided by the East German Communist Party that Cinderella's fairy godmother has no place in one. She has accordingly been eliminated from the orthodox version. Other characters affected by this purge include the king, who has been "unmasked as a witless minor despot"; members of his court, who are revealed as "decadent parasites"; and the prince, who, as "a revolutionary who rejects his previous fruitless parasitic existence," is improved out of all recognition. It is not clear what has happened to the Ugly Sisters; perhaps they were so beastly already that they were spared the wholesome influence of revision.

The main problem in imposing the Party line on fairy stories and nursery rhymes is, one imagines, to know where to stop. The pictures of feudal, or capitalist society which they present are often so devastating—

> The King was in his counting-house,
> Counting out his money;
> The Queen was in her parlour,
> Eating bread and honey—

that by the time they have been reorientated and given a correct perspective what is left really amounts to a sort of atrocity story, calculated to make only a limited appeal to the more sensitive type of young ideologist. Looking ahead to the era, hitherto so aggravatingly delayed, when the revolution shall have triumphed in these islands, it is difficult to think of any harder task which will confront the People's Ministry of Culture than that of sorting out the plots of pantomimes.

London Times, May 29, 1955.

collected in Scotland in the last century, relates to similar tales of wronged orphan girls all over the world, but it has particular Scottish resonances and emphases—this Cinderella meets her prince at the kirk, not the palace. Of course there are fairy tales unique to a single place, which have not been passed on. But there are few really compelling ones that do not turn out to be wearing seven-league boots. The possibility of holding a storehouse of narrative in common could act to enhance our reciprocal relations, to communicate across spaces and barricades of national self-interest and pride. We share more than we perhaps admit or know, and have done so for a very long time: early in the fifteenth century, when Richard, Earl of Warwick, made a pilgrimage to the Holy Land, an emir asked him if he were descended from Guy of Warwick, that celebrated hero of Arthurian romance, whom he had read about 'in bokes of their langage'. The late twentieth century has been seeing a radical reappraisal of such universally known tales—the Grimm Brothers proclaimed their fairy stories the pure uncontaminated national products of the *Volk* or German people, but we now know that many of their tales had been travelling through the world for centuries before the Grimms took them down.

ANOTHER WAY OF SEEING THE WORLD

The balance between popular taste and democratic representation poses one of the most urgent questions facing all the narrative arts, performance and broadcasting as well as literature, for adults and children alike, but it seems a simple admission of defeat to weep and gnash one's teeth at the thought of Euro Disney (a 'cultural Chernobyl', grieved the French philosopher Alain Finkielkraut); it is simply unthinking and lazy to denounce all the works of Disney and his legacy. Theme parks and popular entertainment quarry the tradition of fairy tale—from *Snow White and the Seven Dwarfs* (one of the largest grossing films ever, and still earning) to the recent *Hook* and *Aladdin;* they rely not only on the characters and stories, but on the idea that adults enjoy being children again, that a public can include different generations and classes, who will lose themselves in the make-believe in a different way, united by the pleasures of enchantment. Fairy tales are indeed still criticized—and with reason—for the easy lies, the crass materialism, the false hopes they hold out, but in the last decade of the century, in conditions of radical change on the one hand, and stagnation on the other, with ever increasing fragmentation and widening polarities, with national borders disappearing in some places and returning with a bloody vengeance in others, as a millenarian feeling of ecological catastrophe gathers momentum, and the need to belong grows ever more rampant as it becomes more frustrated, there has been a strongly marked shift towards fantasy as a mode of understanding, as an ingredient in survival, as a lever against the worst aspects of the status quo and the direction it is taking.

Many characteristics of fairy tale as a tradition have contributed to this change: first, the stories' fallaciousness, the very quality that inspired scorn, makes them potential conduits of another way of seeing the world, of telling an alternative story. The mythical hope they conjure actually builds a mythology in which utopian desires find their place. Fairy tales often attack received ideas: monsters turn out to be handsome young princes, beggars princesses, ugly old women powerful and benevolent fairies (especially if you are nice to them and give them something to eat and do their laundry without a fuss). Fairy tales often champion lost causes, runts of the litter, the slow-witted and the malformed. An analogy would be the maxim of the Czech dissidents before the Velvet revolution: Live as if the freedoms you desire were yours already. Only by refusing the constraints that are imposed can they be broken—this is also true of imagining another life, making a new world.

Fairy tales feel out the rules: the forbidden door opens on to *terra nova* where different rules may apply. Curiosity, so closely linked to speech, runs live electricity through many of the stories, and though the questor (Psyche, Bluebeard's wife, Goldilocks) is often punished for not abiding by the rules, the story also runs against its own grain by rewarding her just the same. Since the first medieval romances, with their fairies and monsters, the unreal settings and impossible situations have made possible the exploration of sexual experience and sexual fantasy. One of the chief tropes by which approaches to this forbidden territory are negotiated is animal metamorphosis: confronting or defining the outlawed and alien literally affects the figures in the stories; the beastly or less than human becomes an index of alienation, and often of one's own otherness; the story relates the possibility of acceptance, an end to the ache of longing to belong.

DANGERS OF STANDARDIZING FAIRY TALES

The domain of fantasy where fairy tales grow has a long, heterodox pedigree, and there has been in history a prolonged struggle between different social groups to control the storyteller. The genre's fortunes have entered a new phase: a certain view of fairy tales is being naturalized by companies like Disney, and then domesticated by publishers like Ladybird Books, who have now struck a deal with Disney so that all the illustrations are based on the films' graphics and storyline. The voices whom Calvino heard, for instance, risk being lost in the noise of these loud standard numbers, with certain prejudices and values deeply instilled. This is one of the prima facie problems of corporate reach in the global village: in the same way as hedgerows are shedding variety of species, flora and fauna, the imagination of children reared on Ladybird fairy tales will be saturated with the Disney version, graphic and verbal.

This process of loss has to be resisted: as individual women's voices have become absorbed into the corporate body of male-dominated decision-makers, the misogyny present in many fairy stories—the wicked stepmothers, bad fairies, ogresses, spoiled princesses, ugly sisters and so forth—has lost its connections to the particular web of tensions in which women were enmeshed and come to look dangerously like the way things are. The historical context of the stories has been sheared away, and figures like the wicked stepmother have grown into archetypes of the human psyche, hallowed, inevitable symbols, while figures like the Beast bridegroom have been granted ever more positive status. Generally speaking, the body of story has passed out of the mouth of the quiltmaker from Palermo, on to the lips of film-makers—Steven Spielberg—or psychoanalysts—Bruno Bettelheim—or therapists—Robert Bly. The danger of women has become more and more part of the story, and correspondingly, the danger of men has receded: Cinderella's and Snow White's wicked stepmothers teach children to face life's little difficulties, it is argued, but films about a Bluebeard or a child murderer, as in 'Tom Thumb', are rated Adults Only.

There are grounds for profound pessimism about the narrative possibilities that remain. Yet fairy tale provides motifs in common, a sign language and an image store which can be interpreted and re-interpreted, as many contemporary artists and writers are now doing, from Robert Coover's fictional reworking of 'Pinocchio', to Salman Rushdie's *Haroun and the Sea Stories,* an amalgam of *Sinbad* with *The Wizard of Oz* as well as his own personal trials; to Jeanette Winterson's experimental novels. Among artists, Paula Rego has continued to explore conflicts and tenderness within families and between the sexes using the shared terms of nonsense verses, and new fairy tales like *Peter Pan;* the Quay Brothers, with *The Comb* (1991) and *Institute Benjamenta* (1994), inspired by Robert Walser's *Snow White* and other writings, and Joanna Woodward, in *Princess Brooch and the Sinful Clasp* (1981), have used a mixture of live action and animation to dramatize psychological discovery and erotic adventure in a true fairytale spirit of 'insatiable curiosity'.

THE POWER OF ENCHANTMENT

The idea of awakening, sometimes erotic but not exclusively, goes to the heart of fairy tale's function. But Sleeping Beauty's angle of vision, when she opens her eyes, is different from the point of view of the prince. Of course Italo Calvino, [British author] Angela Carter, and the new executives of The Disney Corporation did not imagine a similar world or indeed see it in a similar way—but they would agree that the uses of enchantment are extremely powerful, and that what is expressed and what is denied, what is discovered and what is rejected, form a picture of the possible world to which Sleeping Beauty, say, will be waking up.

Who tells the story, who recasts the characters and changes the tone becomes very important: no story is ever the same as its source or model, the chemistry of narrator and audience changes it. Karel Čapek puts it valiantly:

> Every narration is a creative and superlatively free story-creating activity . . . I cannot conceal my satisfaction that the word *'epos'* [epic] in its origin means, and in truth is, the spoken word.

Angela Carter puts the same thought more modestly:

> Ours is a highly individualized culture, with a great faith in the work of art as a unique one-off, and the artist as an orig-

inal, a godlike and inspired creator of unique one-offs. But fairy tales are not like that, nor are their makers. Who first invented meatballs? In what country? Is there a definitive recipe for potato soup? Think in terms of the domestic arts. 'This is how I make potato soup.'

Both Čapek and Carter have written 'marvellous tales' of their own which defy rules of sexual and social conduct in a spirit aglow with mischief. Čapek's simple honest peasant comes into a fortune, but does not get to marry the princess and become a king because he loses it all through a hole in his pocket.

The French thinker Félix Guattari, in a powerful historical essay, has asked some fundamental questions about the direction in which the [twentieth] century and its achievements in technology are taking us; he calls for a new vitality in the relations between individuals and the language of the culture they inhabit: 'Unconscious figures of power and knowledge are not universals. They are tied to reference myths profoundly anchored in the psyche, but they can still swing around toward liberatory paths/voices.' He too sketches the possibility of a utopia, dreaming of 'transforming this planet—a living hell for over three quarters of its population—into a universe of creative enchantments'.

The store of fairy tales, that blue chamber where stories lie waiting to be rediscovered, holds out the promise of just those creative enchantments, not only for its own characters caught in its own plotlines; it offers magical metamorphoses to the one who opens the door, who passes on what was found there, and to those who hear what the storyteller brings. The faculty of wonder, like curiosity, can make things happen; it is time for wishful thinking to have its due.

Fairy Tales Are Cathartic

Jane Yolen

In the following article Jane Yolen draws on her experiences as a writer of fairy tales to explain the cathartic effect of the tales. Through the use of symbolic language and archetypes, the simple stories convey to the listener far more than can be comprehended by the rational mind. The impact can be to deliver a particular truth which forces an awakening, or opening to new awareness. A truly potent kind of magic, fairy tales comfort and nurture deep sorrow or awaken the reader to buried hopes and dreams. Fairy tales don't describe actual events, but of far greater significance, the underlying universal truth.

Every few decades, with a regularity that suggests a natural cycle, the fairy tale haters arrive. Under the banner of reason, they blast away with their howitzers at the little singing bird of faerie.

Ever since St. Jerome, who considered such poetic stuff "the food of demons," the haters have played their off-key tune, trying to pipe Pan out of the garden. And whether it was [nineteenth-century British writer and educator] Mrs. Trimmer warning against "the danger as well as the impropriety of putting such books in the hands of little children whose minds are susceptible of every impression . . ." or the well-meaning Gradgrind who wrote in the 1960s in the *London Times Literary Supplement* that fairy stories "ultimately contribute to a more general alienation, a preference for living wholly in dreams and an inability to face reality," the legionnaires of reason have been marching on the right track but in the wrong direction. They would have us believe, as in the old Danish nursery rhyme:

Excerpted from *Touch Magic: Fantasy, Faerie, and Folklore in the Literature of Childhood* (Philomel Books: New York, 1981) by Jane Yolen. Reprinted with permission from Curtis Brown, Ltd.

Oh it is not the fault of the hen
That the cock is dead,
It is the fault of the nightingale
Within the green garden.

The wrong singer is blamed. It is quite definitely *not* the nightingale, the sweet singer, who contributes to alienation. Point the finger, instead, at those down-to-earth hen stories that claim to be about the here-and-now but are, however, so unlike anyone's true existence that they can mislead and misrepresent real life to a reader.

A History of Humankind

It is true that fairy tales have an effect, but it is a healthy, nurturing, cathartic effect, not a fault. Using archetypes and symbolic language, they externalize for the listener conflicts and situations that cannot be spoken of or explained or as yet analyzed. They give substance to dreams.

Folklore is, in part, the history of humankind. And we share fears, hopes, joys with our apelike ancestors who prayed to the sun and hid from the stars. As [novelist] Ursula Le Guin has written, ". . . we all have the same kind of dragons in our psyche, just as we all have the same kind of hearts and lungs in our body."

Folklore is, of course, imperfect history because it is history constantly transforming and being transformed, putting on, chameleonlike, the colors of its background. But while it is imperfect history, it is the perfect guidebook to the human psyche; it leads us to the understanding of the deepest longings and most daring visions of humankind.

The images from the ancients speak to us in modern tongue though we may not always grasp the "meanings" consciously. Like dreams, the meanings slip away, leaving us shaken into new awarenesses. We are moved by them even when—or perhaps *because*—we do not understand them on the conscious level. They are penumbral, partially lit, and it is the dark side that has the most power.

Creating the Literary Fairy Tale

So when the modern mythmaker, the writer of literary fairy tales, dares to touch the old magic and try to make it work in new ways, it must be done with the surest of touches. It is, perhaps, a kind of artistic thievery, this stealing of old characters, settings, the accoutrements of magic. But, then, in a sense, there is an element of theft in all art; even the most imaginative artist borrows and reconstructs the archetypes when delving into the human heart. That is not to say that using a familiar character from folklore in hopes of shoring up a weak narrative will work. That makes little sense. Unless the image, character, or situation borrowed speaks to the author's condition, as cryptically and oracularly as a dream, folklore is best left untapped.

[An] example from my own stories may serve to demonstrate the blending of folkloric elements with original themes to create the literary or art tale.

The Bird of Time is such a collage. I began the story when I misheard some rock lyrics. It was related also to a distant memory of the *Rubáiyát of Omar Khayyám* I had been given as a child, with the multifaceted pictures by Edmund Dulac.

Come into the fire of Spring
Your winter garment of repentance fling.
The bird of time has but a little way to flutter,
And lo! the bird is on the wing.

The story has a traditional son setting out to seek his traditional fortune. Every folk culture boasts numbers of such tales. In my story the hero was also able to understand the language of beasts and birds. You can find such prodigies aplenty in folklore: the Norwegian lad in "The Giant Who Had No Heart in His Body" is one; the Bulgarian boy in "The Snake King's Gift" and the German hero of "Faithful John" (one of my childhood favorites) are others.

But *The Bird of Time* also had a theme of my own devising, and the theme came straight out of my own life. It happened that I began the story when my beloved mother was dying of cancer. In fact, the very day when I wrote the first words of the tale was the day I learned of her condition. Yet such is the ability of the subconscious mind to work out trauma, I did not realize this coincidence of time until months later.

In the story I wrote of a wonder: a bird that could magically alter time, slowing it down, speeding it up, or stopping time altogether. If I could not do such a thing in real life to save my mother, I could certainly do it where I had total control: on the pages of a book.

Months later, when the story was done, I let my mother read the tale in manuscript. (She was not to live to see the finished book, which was dedicated to her.) Only then did I learn how much of me was in the story. I can still see her as she was that day, a small, intense, dark-haired woman sitting in a large brown leather chair. Her legs were curled up under her, her favorite reading position. And when she finished reading, she looked up at me over her glasses and said, "Intimations of mortality, eh?" And smiled.

It was then I knew that she knew she was dying, though my father had been desperate to keep the fact of her cancer from her. And I knew, for the first time, what my little story was all about. . . .

FINDING ONE'S TRUTH IN FAIRY TALE FORM

Diane Wolkstein, who is a great storyteller, has written that when she tells stories to an audience she knows that not every story will strike that kind of chord with every listener. But she can tell, just by the faces, when she has hit *the* story for a particular person. And that is because the listener is immobilized, paralyzed by hearing his or her particular truth being spoken aloud.

These are the kinds of tales that force a confrontation with the deepest kind of reality. In Tolkien's words, these tales give the child "the very taste of primary truth."

I have seen this healing and revealing power of folktale demonstrated clearly within the context of my own family. Our cat Pod, a beautiful golden tom, was killed, rather brutally, by unleashed dogs running wild in our field. The children witnessed the whole thing, and by the time I was able to drive the dogs off, and gather my children, Pod was dead. His golden fur was muddy and mauled, his eyes wide, his once lithe body stiff.

We made an elaborate funeral with singing and prayers and wildflowers to cover him: milkweed fluff and Quaker ladies, Queen Anne's lace, king devil, and rye. We sang him a farewell song and Heidi and Jason, ages ten and six, were able to sob their goodbyes.

But Adam, then age eight, was stony-faced. It was not that he had loved Pod any more or any less. He just would not come to Pod's grave. And he could not cry.

For two days he remained unreachable, his grief held behind a set jaw. He would not talk about it, he barely ate, he would not play with the others. And he could not cry.

The second evening I sat down with the three to read them a fairy tale, one that I loved: the Grimms' story, "Goose Girl," a Cinderella variant. In it, the girl's magical companion, the horse Falada, is ritually killed and its head is hung up over the arched gateway to advise her. As the goose girl walks under the door, she looks up and cries out, "Alas, Falada, hanging there."

When I reached that point in the tale, Adam burst into tears. He sobbed for a long time. And when at last he calmed down, he asked me, "Why can I cry at that story when I couldn't at Pod's death?"

Why indeed? I told him that it had to do with that inner core of "primary truth," only I didn't put it exactly that way. I told him that though life and art are not really imitations, one of another, they resonate. At that particular moment in his particular young life, Adam had found *his* tale.

FAIRY TALES AND LONGING

C.S. Lewis, known for his popluar children's books including
The Lion, the Witch, and the Wardrobe, *defends fairy tales as a worthy form of children's literature in his article "On Three Ways of Writing for Children." In the following extract, he asserts that more realistic fiction can encourage children to be envious and frustrated, whereas fairy tales take the child to a wistful world where deep longings are satisfied in the imagination.*

Do fairy tales teach children to retreat into a world of wish-fulfilment—'fantasy' in the technical psychological sense of the word—instead of facing the problems of the real world? Now it is here that the problem becomes subtle. Let us lay the fairy tale side by side with the school story or any other story which is labelled a 'Boy's Book' or a Girl's Book', as distinct from a 'Children's Book.' There is no doubt that both arouse, and imaginatively satisfy, wishes. We long to go through the looking-glass, to reach fairyland. We also long to be the immensely popular and successful schoolboy or schoolgirl, or the lucky boy or girl who discovers the spy's plot or rides the horse that none of the cowboys can manage. But the two longings are very different. The second, especially when directed on something so close as school life, is ravenous and deadly serious. Its fulfilment on the level of imagination is in very truth compensatory: we run to it from the disappointments and humiliations of the real world; it sends us back to the real world undivinely discontented. For it is all flattery to the ego. The pleasure consists in picturing oneself the object of admi-

Did I know all this before I chose that story? A little, perhaps. I was a mother and a storyteller, and also a bit desperate to reach my child.

All I know is that after that, Adam went outside to the cat's grave that he had dared not visit before.

ACTUALITY AND TRUTH

Falada was not real and Pod was. Yet within the body of the story was a truth that spoke out loud and clear to one grieving little boy. It reminds me, years later, of the truth about dinosaurs and dragons.

Though we are just now finding out that the dinosaur was probably a warm-blooded beast and not the cold-blooded lizard of the textbooks, we have never been in doubt about

---

ration. The other longing, that for fairyland, is very different. In a sense a child does not long for fairyland as a boy longs to be the hero of the first eleven. Does anyone suppose that he really and prosaically longs for all the dangers and discomforts of a fairy tale?—really wants dragons in contemporary England? It is not so. It would be much truer to say that fairyland arouses a longing for he knows not what. It stirs and troubles him (to his lifelong enrichment) with the dim sense of something beyond his reach and, far from dulling or emptying the actual world, gives it a new dimension of depth. He does not despise real woods because he has read of enchanted woods: the reading makes all real woods a little enchanted. This is a special kind of longing. The boy reading the school story of the type I have in mind desires success and is unhappy (once the book is over) because he can't get it: the boy reading the fairy tale desires and is happy in the very fact of desiring. . . .

The dangerous fantasy is always superficially realistic. The real victim of wishful reverie does not batten on The Odyssey, The Tempest, or The Worm Ouroboros: he (or she) prefers stories about millionaires, irresistible beauties, posh hotels, palm beaches, and bedroom scenes—things that really might happen, that ought to happen, that would have happened if the reader had had a fair chance. For, as I say, there are two kinds of longing. The one is an askesis, a spiritual exercise, and the other is a disease.

C.S. Lewis, *Of Other Worlds*, 1966.

dragons. We know, even without being told, that they were born, nourished, kept alive by human blood and heart and mind. They never were—but always will be. It was Kenneth Grahame who wrote: "The dragon is a more enduring animal than a pterodactyl. I have never yet met anyone who really believed in a pterodactyl; but every honest person believes in dragons—down in the back-kitchen of his consciousness."

Dragons and pterodactyls, actuality has nothing to do with Truth.

Throughout the nineteenth century, there was a great deal of speculation about fairies. One group of anthropologists and folklorists held that there really had been a race of diminutive prehistoric people who had been driven underground by successive invasions. These "little folk," who were really about the size of pygmies, supposedly lived for years in communities in caves and burrows, in warrens and tunnels and in the deepest, darkest parts of the forest where, in brown-and-green camouflage, they stayed apart from their enemies. Kidnapings and mysterious disappearances were all attributed to them. These hardy guerrillas of a defeated culture became, in the folk mind, the elves and gnomes and trolls and fairies of the British Isles. There were even archeologists who were convinced they had discovered rooms underground in the Orkney Islands that resembled the Elfland of the popular ballad *Child Rowland.* (And similarly, other such folk stories might have emerged by a misunderstanding of the weirs and dikes used by the Romans for their household baths.)

It is a very seductive thesis, but it really begs the question. For even if we do conclusively prove that the Picts or Celts or some other smaller-than-average race are the *actual* precursors of the fairy folk, it will not really change a thing about those wonderful stories. The tales of Elfland do not stand or fall on their actuality but on their truthfulness, their speaking to the human condition, the longings we all have for the Faerie Other. Those are the tales that touch our longing for the better, brighter world; our shared myths, our shaped dreams. The fears and longings within each of us that helped us create Heaven and Elysium, Valhalla and Tir nan og.

This is the stuff that dreams are made of. Not the smaller dreams that you and I have each night, rehearsals of things to come, anticipation or dread turned into murky symbols, pastiches of traumas just passed. These are the larger dreams of humankind, a patchwork of all the smaller dreams stitched together by time.

The best of the stories we can give our children, whether they are stories that have been kept alive through the centuries by that mouth-to-mouth resuscitation we call oral transmission, or the tales that were made up only yesterday—the best of these stories touch that larger dream, that greater vision, that infinite unknowing. They are the most potent kind of magic, these tales, for they catch a glimpse of the soul beneath the skin.

Touch magic. Pass it on.

CHRONOLOGY

ca. 100–200

Apuleius's "Cupid and Psyche," considered the first literary fairy tale, is written in Latin

ca. 200–300

Panchatantra, a famous Hindu collection of tales thought to include forerunners of some European fairy tales, is written

850–860

The first datable written record of "Cinderella" is found in China

ca. 1300

Gesta Romanorum, an early collection of anecdotes and tales, including fairy tales, is written in Latin

ca. 1500

One Thousand and One Arabian Nights, fairy and folktales collected from Arabia, Persia, Egypt, and India, is written in Arabic

1550 AND 1553

Gianfrancesco Straparola publishes *Le piacevoli notti (The Pleasant Nights)* in two volumes, the earliest European storybook to include fairy tales

1590–1596

Edmund Spenser writes "The Faerie Queen," the most renowned poem of the Renaissance period in England

1590–1611

Shakespeare's plays *A Midsummer Night's Dream* and *The Tempest* show fairy-tale influence

1634

Giambattista Basile writes *Pentamerone,* which includes the earliest Cinderella tale found in Europe

ca. 1680

Puritan influence in England produces hostility toward amusement and fairy tales; the Puritan influence would last into the next century

1690—1714

Fairy tales come into vogue in the salons of France; the genre is first called *contes de fée,* or fairy tales; theater, ballet, and opera use fairy-tale themes

1696—1698

Marie-Catherine D'Aulnoy, the innovator of fairy tales as a literary genre, publishes four volumes of fairy tales

1697

Charles Perrault's *Histoires du Contes du temps passé* is the first children's book of fairy tales

1704—1717

Antoine Galland translates *One Thousand and One Arabian Nights* into French

1740

Madame de Villeneuve writes "Beauty and the Beast"

ca. 1750

Fairy tales are simplified for chapbooks that are distributed by peddlers to lower classes throughout France

1756

Governess Le Prince de Beaumont's "Beauty and the Beast" solidifies the fairy tale as a form of children's literature

1785

Charles Mayer's *Le Cabinet des Fees* (forty-one volumes of fairy tales) establishes the genre in the Western intellectual tradition

1786

Johann Karl Musäus' *Volksmärchen der Deutschen,* the first German collection of fairy and folktales, is published

1789

French Revolution begins; literary Romanticism takes hold in Europe

1795

Johann Wolfgang Goethe's *The Fairy Tale* serves as a critique of the Enlightenment and the French Revolution

1802

Sarah Trimmer's publication of the magazine *Guardian of Education* in England warns against the negative influence of fairy tales on children

1812 AND 1815

Jacob and Wilhelm Grimm's *Kinder-und Hausmärchen* (*Childhood and Household Tales*) is published and inspires major folklore collections throughout Europe

1819

Washington Irving's *Rip Van Winkle*, the earliest American adaptation of the European fairy tale, is published

1830

Samuel Griswald Goodrich campaigns to ban the *Mother Goose Tales* in the United States

1830–1890

Industrial Revolution takes hold first in Europe, then in America

1835

Hans Christian Andersen's *Fairy Tales Told for Children* is published

1843

Charles Dickens' *A Christmas Carol* is published

1854

Nathaniel Hawthorne's *Feathertop* is published

1859

Peter Christen Asbjørnsen and Jørgen Moe's *Norwegian Folktales* is published

1863

Charles Kingsley's *The Water Babies* is published

1865

Lewis Carroll's *Alice's Adventures in Wonderland* is published

1867

George MacDonald's *Dealings with the Fairies* is published

1883

Carlo Collodi's *Pinocchio* is published

1887

Frank Stockton's *The Bee Man of Orn and Other Fanciful Tales* is published

1888

Oscar Wilde's *The Happy Prince* is published

1889

Andrew Lang's *The Blue Fairy Book* is published

1889

Tchaikovsky's orchestral work "Sleeping Beauty" captures fairy-tale themes abundant in music

1890

Joseph Jacobs' *English Fairy Tales* is published

1892

W.B. Yeats's *Fairy and Folk Tales of Ireland* is published

1900

L. Frank Baum's *The Wonderful Wizard of Oz* is published

1914

World War I begins in Europe

1917

Hermann Hesse's "The Forest Dweller" is published

1918

World War I ends

1924

Thomas Mann's *The Magic Mountain* is published

1929

The Great Depression hits the United States

1937

Walt Disney's film *Snow White and the Seven Dwarfs* is released

1938

J.R.R. Tolkien's *The Hobbit* is published, supposedly with forewarnings of a second world war

1939

World War II begins in Europe; the Nazi Party uses the Grimms' fairy tales to indoctrinate their philosophy of racial superiority

1940

Tales like H.L. Phillips's "Little Red Riding Hood as a Dictator Would Tell Us" are published, representing an American response to the distortions of the Nazi Party's use of the genre

1947

Italo Calvino publishes *Fiabe Italiene,* a collection of Italian tales designed to bridge the gap between the social classes in Italy

1949

Ingeborg Bachmann writes "The Smile of the Sphinx," a fairy tale reflecting the horror of the Holocaust; the Cold War begins; the Marxist rewriting of fairy tales occurs in eastern bloc countries

1950

C.S. Lewis's *The Lion, the Witch, and the Wardrobe* is published

1960s–1970s

Civil rights and feminist movements give rise to debates over and fresh adaptations of fairy tales

1971

Anne Sexton publishes *Transformations,* a collection of poems based on the Grimms' fairy tales

1975

Rosemary Minard's *Womenfolk and Fairy Tales* is published, comprising lesser known tales with strong female heroines

1976

Bruno Bettelheim's *The Uses of Enchantment: The Meaning and Importance of Fairy Tales* is published

1979

Angela Carter's *The Bloody Chamber and Other Tales* rewrites classic tales from a female point of view

1983

Sarah Moon's *Little Red Riding Hood* is published

1983

Tanith Lee's *Red as Blood or Tales from the Sisters Grimmer* is published

1984–1987

Shelley Duvall's televised *Faerie Tale Theatre* represents the regressive tendencies of the genre in the 1980s

1987

Television series *Beauty and the Beast* airs

1988

Jim Henson's *Snow White and the Seven Muppets,* a spoof of Disney's version of the fairy tale, airs on television

1988

Wendy Walker's *The Sea-Rabbit, or the Artist of Life* is published

1990

Tom Davenport's progressive film adaptation of "Cinderella," *Ashpet: An American Cinderella,* is released

1992

Jane Yolen's *Briar Rose* is published; Tom Davenport and Gary Carden's *From the Brothers Grimm: A Contemporary Retelling of American Folktales and Classic Stories* is published

1993

Disney's animated film *Beauty and the Beast* is released

1995

Ellen Datlow and Terri Windling's *Ruby Slippers, Golden Tears,* which includes innovative contemporary revisions of classical fairy tales, is published

1996

Robert Coover's *Briar Rose* is published

1997

Emma Donoghue's *Kissing the Witch: Old Tales in New Skins* is published

1999

Sheldon Cashdan's *The Witch Must Die: How Fairy Tales Shape Our Lives* is published

FOR FURTHER RESEARCH

CLASSICAL EUROPEAN FAIRY TALES

Hans Christian Andersen, *Tales and Stories by Hans Christian Andersen.* Trans. Patricia L. Conroy and Sven. H. Rossel. Seattle: University of Washington Press, 1980.

———, *Tales: English Selections.* Ed. Svend Larsen. Denmark: Flensted, 1950.

Jacob and Wilhelm Grimm, *The Complete Fairy Tales of the Brothers Grimm.* Trans. and ed. Jack Zipes. New York: Bantam, 1987.

———, *The Complete Grimms' Fairy Tales.* New York: Pantheon Books, 1972.

———, *The Complete Household Tales of Jakob and Wilhelm Grimm.* New York: Limited Editions Club; Case, Lockwood, and Brainard, 1962.

Andrew Lang, ed., *The Blue Fairy Book.* 1889. Reprint, New York: Longman's Green, 1948.

Iona and Peter Opie, *The Classic Fairy Tales.* London: Oxford University Press, 1974.

Charles Perrault, *Histories or Tales of Past Times.* New York: Garland, 1977.

FAIRY TALES FROM AROUND THE WORLD

The Arabian Nights. Trans. Husain Haddawy. New York: W.W. Norton, 1990.

Peter Christen Asbjørnsen and Jørgen Moe, eds., *East of the Sun and West of the Moon.* New York: Macmillan, 1963.

Nina Auerbach and U.C. Knoepflmacher, eds., *Forbidden Journeys: Fairy Tales and Fantasies by Victorian Women Writers.* Chicago: University of Chicago Press, 1992.

L. Frank Baum, *The Wizard of Oz.* New York: Penguin, 1982.

Pearl S. Buck, *Fairy Tales of the Orient.* New York: Simon and Schuster, 1965.

Italo Calvino, *Italian Folktales.* Trans. George Martin. New York: Harcourt Brace Jovanovich, 1980.

Angela Carter, ed., *The Old Wives' Fairy Tale Book.* New York: Pantheon Books, 1990.

——, *Strange Thing Sometimes Still Happen: Fairy Tales from Around the World.* Boston: Faber and Faber, 1994.

Virginia Hamilton, *Her Stories: African American Folktales, Fairy Tales, and True Tales.* New York: Blue Sky/Scholastic, 1995.

Joseph Jacobs, *English Fairy Tales.* New York: Putnam's, 1890.

Alison Lurie, ed., *The Oxford Book of Modern Fairy Tales.* Oxford, England: Oxford University Press, 1993.

Rosemary Minard, ed., *Womenfolk and Fairy Tales.* Boston: Houghton, 1975.

Neil Phillip, *American Fairy Tales.* New York: Hyperion, 1996.

Frank R. Stockton, *The Best Stories of Frank R. Stockton.* New York: Scribner, 1957.

Pamela Travers, *About the Sleeping Beauty.* New York: McGraw-Hill, 1975.

W.B. Yeats, *Fairy and Folk Tales of Ireland.* New York: Macmillan, 1973.

Jack Zipes, ed., *Spells of Enchantment: The Wondrous Fairytales of Western Culture.* New York: Viking, 1991.

CONTEMPORARY FAIRY TALES

Angela Carter, *The Bloody Chamber and Other Tales.* London: Gollancz, 1979.

Robert Coover, *Briar Rose.* New York: Grove, 1996.

Ellen Datlow and Terri Windling, edit. *Ruby Slippers, Golden Tears.* New York: William Morrow, 1995.

Tom Davenport and Gary Carden, *From the Brothers Grimm: A Contemporary Retelling of American Folktales and Classic Stories.* Wisconsin: Highsmith, 1992.

Emma Donaghue, *Kissing the Witch: Old Tales in New Skins.* London: Hamish Hamilton, 1997.

Tanith Lee, *Red as Blood or Tales from the Sisters Grimmer.* New York: DAW, 1983.

Wolfgang Mieder, ed. *Disenchantments: An Anthology of Modern Fairy Tale Poetry.* Hanover: University Press of New England, 1985.

Salman Rushdie, *Haroun and the Sea of Stories.* New York: Viking, 1990.

Anne Sexton, *Transformations.* Boston: Houghton Mifflin, 1971.

Wendy Walker, *The Sea-Rabbit, or the Artist of Life.* Los Angeles: Sun and Moon, 1988.

Terri Windling, ed., *The Armless Maiden and Other Tales from Childhood's Survivors.* New York: Tor Books, 1995.

Jane Yolen, *Briar Rose.* New York: Tor Books, 1992.

———, *Dragonfield and Other Stories.* New York: Ace Books, 1985.

———, *Tales of Wonder.* New York: Ace Books, 1983.

Jack Zipes, ed., *Don't Bet on the Prince: Contemporary Feminist Fairy Tales in North America and England.* New York: Methuen, 1986.

ANALYSIS AND CRITICISM OF FAIRY TALES

Bruno Bettelheim, *The Uses of Enchantment: The Meaning and Importance of Fairy Tales.* New York: Alfred A. Knopf, 1976.

Ruth Bottigheimer, ed., *Fairy Tales and Society: Illusion, Allusion, and Paradigm.* Philadelphia: University of Pennsylvania Press, 1986.

———, *Grimms' Bad Girls and Bold Boys: The Moral and Social Vision of the Tales.* New Haven, CT: Yale University Press, 1987.

Sheldon Cashdan, *The Witch Must Die: How Fairy Tales Shape Our Lives.* New York: BasicBooks, 1999.

Robert Darnton, *The Great Cat Massacre and Other Episodes in French Cultural History.* New York: Vintage Books, 1985.

Charles Dickens, "Frauds on the Fairies," in Michael Slater, ed., *The Dent Uniform Edition of Dickens Journalism.* Vol. 3. *Gone Astray and Other Papers from Household Words, 1851–59.* Columbus: Ohio State University Press, 1998.

Alan Dundes, ed., *Cinderella: A Folklore Casebook.* New York: Garland, 1982.

———, *Little Red Riding Hood: A Casebook.* Madison: University of Wisconsin Press, 1989.

Donald Haase, "Feminist Fairy-Tale Scholarship: A Critical Survey and Bibliography," *Marvels and Tales,* April 2000.

———, ed., *The Reception of Grimms' Fairy Tales: Responses, Reactions, Revisions.* Detroit, MI: Wayne State University Press, 1993.

Betsy Hearne, *Beauty and the Beast: Visions and Revisions of an Old Tale.* Chicago: University of Chicago Press, 1989.

———, "Disney Revisited, or Jiminy Cricket, It's Musty Down Here," *Horn Book Magazine,* March/April 1997.

Steven Swann Jones, *The Fairy Tale: The Magic Mirror of Imagination.* New York: Twayne, 1995.

Max Luthi, *The Fairy Tale as Art Form and Portrait of Man.* Bloomington: University of Indiana Press, 1985.

———, *Once upon a Time: On the Nature of Fairy Tales.* New York: Ungar, 1970.

James M. McGlathery, ed., *The Brothers Grimm and the Folktale.* Chicago: University of Illinois Press, 1988.

Vladimir Propp, *Theory and History of Folklore.* Minneapolis: University of Minnesota Press, 1984.

Roger Sale, *Fairy Tales and After: From Snow White to E.B. White.* Cambridge, MA: Harvard University Press, 1978.

Francis Clarke Sayers, "Walt Disney Accused," *Horn Book Magazine,* December, 1965.

Kay F. Stone, "Things Walt Disney Never Told Us," *Journal of American Folklore,* 1975.

Maria Tartar, *The Hard Facts of Grimms' Fairy Tales.* Princeton, NJ: Princeton University Press, 1987.

Stith Thompson, *The Folktale.* New York: Holt, Rhinehart, and Winston, 1946.

J.R.R. Tolkien, *Tree and Leaf.* Boston: Houghton Mifflin, 1965.

Marie-Louise Von Franz, *The Interpretation of Fairy Tales.* Boston: Shambala Publications, 1996.

Marina Warner, *From the Beast to the Blonde: On Fairy Tales and Their Tellers.* London: Chatto and Windus, 1994.

Jane Yolen, *Touch Magic: Fantasy, Faerie, and Folklore in the Literature of Childhood.* New York: Philomel, 1981.

Jack Zipes, *Fairy Tales and the Art of Subversion: The Classical Genre for Children and the Process of Civilization.* New York: Wildman, 1983.

——, *Fairy Tale as Myth/Myth as Fairy Tale.* Lexington: University Press of Kentucky, 1994.

——, *Happily Ever After: Fairy Tales, Children, and the Culture Industry.* New York: Routledge, 1997.

BIOGRAPHIES OF FAIRY-TALE AUTHORS AND COLLECTORS

Hans Christian Andersen, *The Fairy Tale of My Life: An Autobiography.* New York: Paddington, 1975.

Jacques Barchilon and Peter Flinders, *Charles Perrault.* Boston: Twayne, 1981.

Frederik Böök, *Hans Christian Andersen: A Biography.* Norman: University of Oklahoma Press, 1963.

Henry L. Golemba, *Frank R. Stockton.* Boston: Twayne, 1981.

Murray B. Peppard, *Paths Through the Forest; A Biography of Jacob and Wilhelm Grimm.* New York: Holt, Rhinehart, and Winston, 1971.

Charles Perrault, *Charles Perrault, Memoirs of My Life.* ed. and trans. Jeanne Morgan Zarucchi. Columbia: University of Missouri Press, 1989.

Richard Schickel, *The Disney Version: The Life, Times, Art, and Commerce of Walt Disney.* Chicago: Elephant Paperbacks, 1997.

Jack Zipes, *When Dreams Came True: Classical Fairy Tales and Their Tradition.* New York: Routledge, 1999.

WEBSITES

The following websites, provided courtesy of Donald Haase, editor of *Marvels and Tales,* a journal of fairy-tale scholarship, are wonderful introductory sources for fairy-tale scholars. Created and written by groups of college students from around the United States, these sites include basic information and a bibliographical guide on the specified tale or topic. The authors provide e-mail addresses for further contact. The sites may be accessed through the *Marvels and Tales* web links page at www.langlab.wayne.edu/MarvelsHome/links.html.

Children's Literature and Web Guide
(www.acs.ucalgary.ca/-dkbrown/index.html)

Cinderella Bibliography
(http://docserver.ub.rug.n1/camelot/cinder/cin15.htm)

Cinderella Project
(www.dept.usm.edu/-engdept/cinderella/cinderella.html)

French Fairy Tales
(www.wesleyan.edu/fist255s.mle.projects.html)

Grimm Brothers Homepage
(www.pitt.edu/-dash/grimm.html)

Jack and the Beanstalk Project
(www.dept.usm.edu/-engdept/jack/jackhome.html)

Little Red Riding Hood Project
(www.dept.usm.edu/-engdept/lrrh/lrrhhome.html)

Snow White
(www.scils.rutgers.edu/special/kay/snowwhite.html)

INDEX